CELTIC VOICES

Inspirational Monologues

For

Sacred Storytelling / Dramatic Readings

BOBBIE M. PELL

Imaginary Lands

Mars Hill, NC

Cover Photo: Glendalough, Ireland in Wicklow Mountains

[St. Kevin's Monastic Site]

by Bobbie M. Pell

Cover Design: Glenda Owens

Interior Photos by Bobbie Pell

ISBN: 9781793062116 (pbk)

DEDICATIONS

This book is dedicated to my Episcopal priest, Rev. David McNair, who after enjoying my participation in a Sacred Feminine service where I portrayed Mary Magdalene, asked the pregnant question, "So, do you do any other saints?" To which I replied, "Not yet, but there may be some in my future!"

ACKNOWLEDGMENTS

To my fabulous readers Saundra G. Kelley and Nancy Napier, I once again give you thanks for your technical precision, careful considerations, and constant faith in my writing abilities!

To my husband Ron, my heart is filled with the steadfastness of your soul as your life inspires me to continuously move forward!

TABLE OF CONTENTS

PART ONE: MONOLOGUE TIPS

PART TWO: THE GOLDEN AGE OF CELTIC CHRISTIANITY

PART THREE: MONOLOGUES

MONOLOGUE TIPS

INTENTION

The purpose of this book is to open the pathway for professional storytellers, performers, lay worship leaders, and ministers/parish priests to walk beside Celtic spiritual leaders of the past and share their amazing feats of faith. The Celtic saints represented in this collection show fierce determination in the face of adversity, kindness and generosity for their fellow man, and intuitive connections with both the spiritual realms and the natural world. These sketches provide biographical information, legends, amazing miracles, wondrous encounters, and angelic support. Each work contains an original monologue paired with insightful prayers and poems from the wonderful collection of Alexander Carmichael, Carmina Gaedelica (public domain, 1900) and supportive hymn verses.

For those simply interested in Celtic Spirituality, this book is also for you! You will watch miracles such as mantles (cloaks) spreading for miles to set boundaries of a new monastic site, sea serpents defeated, animals rescuing psalters, and even shape-shifting episodes from human to animal forms! These tales, based on true life events, will simply amaze you!

CHOICE OF SAINTS

Seven saints, whose lives reflect varied spiritual practices, were specifically chosen to create a diverse collection. When considering how many saints to include, I recalled the symbolism related to numbers, an ideal often reflected in early Celtic prayers and teachings. Ancient Celts believed the number three to represent wholeness and unity, reflected in book art illuminations through the use of triad knot patterns. Three also refers to both the Holy Trinity (Father, Son, Holy Spirit) and the triune gods/goddesses during pagan times. By adding the number four, symbolizing the cardinal directions (north, east, south, west) and the primary elements in nature (earth, air, water, fire) to the triads of three, we arrive at the sacred number of seven, the joining of heaven and earth.

The "Biblical Bonus Section" containing a monologue by Mary Magdalene is where this collection first began, so it felt only fitting to include it here.

TIME ALLOWANCE

Each monologue easily fits into a weekend Storytelling Event for Sacred Telling on Sunday mornings or olio sessions, running approximately twenty minutes. These works can also be inserted into the Order of Service for the homily/sermon slot during a traditional church service. They may be performed (without notes) or shared as Dramatic Readings (with notes).

DELIVERY STYLES

The monologues were created for flexibility in delivery styles. I employed phrases and wording in line with the country of origin for the saint, so if you are comfortable with a British or Irish accent, feel free. If not, simply read the work aloud with clear enunciations, applying emotional flavor, pauses, and pitch variances to add an appropriate sense of drama to the scenes. Be sure to read through the monologues first to gain a feel for the work as a whole piece then review it several more times, highlighting and making notes for yourself. The text has wide margins and convenient line spacing for just this purpose.

In writing each monologue, I conducted careful research and prayerful meditations then waited to hear the natural cadences of each person portrayed. As a fiction writer, I often hear the "voices" of my characters through their word choice, imagery, and flow of language; the same process proved true for these works. I infused my own spiritual beliefs through the angle of perspective in each piece in line with what I discovered about the personality of each saint.

CLOTHING

For performers, you may wish to research styles of monastic robes and women's "habits" of the early church. I was amazed that simply by layering black and white clothing, I suddenly became Saint Julian, to the point that I was unrecognizable by my own congregation! If you wish for authenticity, hand-woven monk habits from India (one size fits all) can be obtained under "Costumes" on Amazon.

For those conducting Dramatic Readings, you may wish to simply dress appropriately for the venue in comfortable clothing. Perhaps your choice of attire can reflect ideas you connect with in the monologue. I portrayed Saint Brighid in this way, wearing a long white dress with a lavender scarf since she was supportive of the arts and imagination. You may read directly from the book or add a fictional opener about how this "series of personal letters" or "diary" was found and how you now wish to share it. For instance, I printed the monologue then placed it between two sheets of hand-made paper, binding it with ribbon. The delivery was just as effective!

EXPANDING THE TIME FRAME

If you wish to expand the monologue for longer venues (forty-five - sixty minutes), simply add any prayers, psalms, Celtic poetry/blessings, or hymns between sections. You can also include the audience/congregation for "Call and Response" poems/blessings, communal songs, and open prayer. I invite you to seek ways that aid in making the monologue your own. If you are paid for the performance, be sure to use materials from the public domain (copyright free); if you select materials currently under copyright, simply request permission. If you wish to use any of my monologues for reproduction (DVD, CD), digital duplication, or public recordings, you must contact me for negotiated permission.

To check the status of hymns, consult the following website: www.hymnary.org.

CELEBRATED FEAST DAYS

Each of the saints represented in this book are celebrated annually in several sectors: Episcopal, Roman Catholic, and Earth-based religions. An easy fit into a church's calendar for performances/dramatic readings would be near the feast day of a specific saint. Below find the saints studied in this book with their annual feast day for your convenience

May 15: Brendan the Navigator

Feb. 1: Brighid, Foster Mother of Christ

March 1: David of Wales

March 17: Patrick, Patron Saint of Ireland

May 8: Julian of Norwich

June 3: Kevin of Glendalough

Sept. 9: Ciaran of Clonmacnoise

July 22: Mary Magdalene

ENJOYMENT OF SHARING

As a consummate storyteller now of over thirty-five years, I must say that taking on the personae of these phenomenal individuals is powerful! You are not simply telling a story; you are sharing a faith-filled life. You invite your audience to share this journey, meeting them on all three planes simultaneously: mental, emotional, and spiritual. By saying these words in first person, the performance allows the teller/reader to open their own hearts to the truths they share. Slainte!

THE GOLDEN AGE OF CELTIC CHRISTIANITY

HISTORICAL OVERVIEW

Imagine yourself standing in the center of an oak grove, a complete circle of trees surrounding you with their mighty leafless limbs stretching effortlessly towards a cerulean sky. Clumps of mistletoe adorn their branches while scampering squirrels burrow within their channeled trunks, feasting on winter stores. A cold wind reminds you that another solstice has passed, bringing in the new year, so now is a time of reflection. Allow yourself to feel the earth steadily supporting you, grounding you in the principles of nature. Inhale slowly; breathe deeply. Allow the cool air to fill your lungs with invigorating life. By attuning yourself to the natural world, you join thousands of pilgrims before you who sought their spirituality from these connections alone until the man Jesus announced his intentions to the world. Celtic Christianity is a seamless blending of the ancient earth-based beliefs with the tenets of Christ, neither philosophy exclusive of the other.

From a historical perspective, the growth of the early Celtic Church expanded between fifth through twelfth centuries ("The

Golden Age"). Ironically, this system of faith paralleled the period known as "The Dark Ages" in the following regions of Europe: England, Ireland, Scotland, Brittany, Wales, and Isle of Man. Monastic life encouraged friendship among the early saints, valued artistic expression (Illuminated Book Arts, poetry, use of the imagination), and learned Divine teachings inspired by stories and dreams. Possible roots in Christianity came from either the Apostle Paul and Apostle Peter (in their travels) or Joseph of Arimathea, believed to have visited Glastonbury. As the flower of Christianity bloomed, monastic sites dotted hillsides and remote villages, bringing the love of Christ to pagan followers. Their acceptance of the scriptures and the doctrines of faith allowed believers to embrace these new practices with their previous ones, believing the True God was All-Encompassing, vast enough to hold all. These small churches became central to village life while their leaders also prompted missionary outreach.

Most monastic sites offered residential studies for men while women attended nearby nunneries where both groups joined in common worship. They shared the fruit of their gardens for food, herbal teas and remedies to avert illness, and livestock such as sheep, goats, and cows. Living accommodations and daily chores were kept separate.

One common problem throughout the provinces arose in the form of violence and fear. Craftsmen were encouraged to create Eucharistic mass items such as chalices and patens (plates) along with decorative boxes for illuminated texts. These works of art, often encrusted with gems, were traditionally created in silver and gold. These treasures were often stolen by northern Vikings in vicious raids until the end of the 9th century. To find safety from these invaders, most sites built tall, stone towers such as the Round Tower at Ireland's Clonmacnoise (18' in diameter, 62' in height) with a stone doorway located twelve to fifteen feet above the ground. A rope ladder was left hanging for easy access, so that when the monks were under attack, they ascended the ladder with haste then pulled it up behind them. An interior spiral staircase led to various levels of wooden floors to provide a safe haven. Small rooms filled with food stores allowed sustenance for the monks while under siege. The conical top bore four windows as lookouts, facing the four cardinal directions.

A core system of beliefs connected these early Celtic Christians. First and foremost was their sound trust in God the Creator, accepting the wonders of the natural world. For those born within an agrarian society whose very lives were daily ruled by seasons in accordance with solar and lunar turnings, this comes as no surprise. "Wise women" shared their knowledge of herbal lore with those for a heart to learn. This knowledge fostered invaluable ties between healers and "miracle makers."

By learning from the solitudes in nature, Celtic Christians also bonded with the animal world in gentle, often reciprocal relationships. Such is evident in the lives of St. Ciaran, when he found aid from a wild boar while attempting to clear land for a new monastic site, along with St. Kevin, where milk was provided for an orphaned infant by a nursing deer. By acknowledging certain qualities connected with a specific animal, believers sought insights into daily struggles when an encounter with an animal occurred.   This line of thought is common amongst agrarian tribal or clan societies. A list of sacred animals and their attributes is given below as recorded in <u>Druid Animal Oracle</u> (Phillip and Stephanie Carr-Gomm):

ADDER: Transformation, Healing, Life Energy

BEAR: Primal Power, Sovereignty, Intuition

BEE: Community, Celebration, Organization

BLACKBIRD: Enchantment, Gateway, Inner Call

BOAR: Warrior, Leadership, Direction

BULL: Wealth, Potency, Beneficence

CAT: Guardianship, Detachment, Sensuality

COW: Nourishment, Motherhood, The Goddess

CRANE: Secret Knowledge, Patience, Longevity

DOG: Guidance, Protection, Loyalty

AIR DRAGON: Inspiration, Insight, Vitality

EARTH DRAGON: Power, Potential, Riches

FIRE DRAGON: Transmutation, Mastery, Energy

WATER DRAGON: Passion, Depth, Connection

EAGLE: Intelligence, Renewal, Courage

FOX: Cunning, Diplomacy, Wildness

FROG: Sensitivity, Medicine, Hidden Beauty/Power

GOOSE: Vigilance, Parenthood, Productive Power

HARE: Rebirth, Intuition, Balance

HAWK: Nobility, Recollection, Cleansing

HIND: Subtlety, Gracefulness, Femininity

HORSE: The Goddess, The Land, Travel

OTTER: Joy, Play, Helpfulness

OWL: Detachment, Wisdom, Change

RAM: Sacrifice, Breakthrough, Achievement

RAVEN: Healing, Initiation, Protection

SALMON: Wisdom, Inspiration, Rejuvenation

SEAL: Love, Longing, Dilemma

SOW: Generosity, Nourishment, Discovery

STAG: Pride, Independence, Purification

SWAN: Soul, Love, Beauty

WOLF: Intuition, Learning, The Shadow

WREN: Humility, Cunning, God

Such beliefs added layers of personal understanding and a natural flavor to daily life.

Additional characteristics which colored the early Celtic Christian Church were scholarly pursuits and mentor relationships. Believers exhibited a love of silence and the lessons taught through solitude. These heart teachings were practiced in everyday responsibilities, each act conducted in gratitude, joy, and kinship. To spread these values abroad, "wanderlust" was offered a new name: missions. The desire to travel became a third style of monastic devotion denoting the intention of travel:

1) "Red martyrdom" - giving up your life for Christ

2) "Green martyrdom" - severe penitent rituals

3) "White martyrdom" - living years from home for Christ's sake.

Despite conflicts with the early Roman Church, this church flourished for hundreds of years. However, administrators between the Holy Church of Rome and these smaller sites came to a head at the Synod of Whitby in 664 where tensions rose due to various differences in their primary practices. Still, this Celtic Church survived until it became assimilated into the Roman Church by the 12th century.

For additional information on this topic, please consult **"APPENDIX:RESOURCES"** section, particularly these two books: Edward Sellner's <u>Wisdom of the Celtic Saints</u> and Timothy Joyce's <u>Celtic Christianity.</u>

PRIMARY CELTIC FEAST DAYS

One wonderful way of blending old and new beliefs was seen in the continuance of the practices welcoming the four primary feast days. Each festival is celebrated on the eve before the first day of the month:

Samhain (Winter): November, December January

Imbolc: (Spring): February, March, April

Beltane (Summer): May, June, July

Lughansadh (Fall): August, September, October.

Each festival honored specific ideals through songs, dances, and activities:

Samhain: rest, ancestral communion, introspection

Imbolc: sprouting, beginnings, primal innocence

Beltane: fertility, burgeoning, creative expression

Lughnasadh: fruiting, maturity, consolidation.

Many of the saints condoned these early traditions, building upon ancient beliefs while offering the teachings of Christ. These ancient celebrations are the roots of our modern festivities today.

OVERVIEW OF THE SAINTS

Brendan the Navigator (486-578 AD)

Saint Brendan dwelled on the Dingle Peninsula along the cold, Atlantic waters on the west coast of Ireland. As a boy, a prophecy was declared, instructing Brendan to venture west. Following his monastic studies, Brendan boarded a small, single-masted curragh (wooden boat) along with several brethren in search of the Isle of Paradise, so that men may believe in the wonders of God. He traveled for seven years, encountering sea monsters, gryphons, ageless men, and birds that could speak. His request to locate the Isle of Paradise was granted, so upon returning home, he lived out the rest of days on the Dingle Peninsula where he established studies at the Clonfert Monastery.

Brighid of Kildare (452-524 AD)

Brighid of Kildare is considered by some to be an incarnation of the goddess Brigit. The two women shared such qualities as poetry, smithcraft (hearth), imagination, and healing. As a babe in the womb then later in the cradle, Brighid's connection with fire showed itself to be significant, and remained so throughout her life. Her legends of creating abundance out of scarcity relate to specific incidents with milk, cows, bacon, wine, and even land! To the ancient Celts, they also believed her to be the Foster Mother of Christ, having been miraculously spirited away on the eve of Christ's birth to attend Mary as a midwife. Her monastic site in Kildare, Ireland still contains the actual fire pit which she herself attended, and until the Reformation, nuns honored this saint's passing by maintaining the "Flame of Brighid."

David of Wales (520-589 AD)

David represents a man in close connection with nature, especially the element of water, having been birthed near the sea. His many incidents with animals showed a quiet man, one in tune with the cycles of life. He set up a monastic site under the new Benedictine Rule, exhibiting a balance of study, worship, and daily chores. The setting was austere to some, yet the lack of distractions allowed the saint and his followers to delve more deeply into a singleness of devotion.

Patrick, Patron Saint of Ireland (390-461 AD)

One of the most well-known saints, Patrick, was born in Britain despite being claimed by Ireland in later years as its Patron Saint. Early childhood reveals that age sixteen, Patrick was kidnapped and sold into slavery where he served in Antrim, Ireland. He remained there for seven years until a pathway to freedom opened. How ironic that once he completed his monastic studies, Patrick returned to Ireland with a new vision, a new mission. He established the first monastic site in Armagh and confronted even the High King Loeguire himself. It was prophesied then that the flame Patrick brought would never be put out. His miraculous strength and powers were tested against Druids, kings, and pagans alike. Yet his gentle spirit, relentless faith, and fierce protests to injustices won the people over to his precepts about Christ. His popularity was unparalleled.

Julian of Norwich (1342-1412 AD)

Julian of Norwich, early anchoress of the Roman Church, revealed a singular dedication to sharing her visions and near-death experiences with the world. At the age of thirty, she prayed to know the bodily pains of Christ, to become so ill she teetered on the brink of death in order to be purged then healed, and last, to be given the gifts of contrition, compassion, and steadfast longing for God. Her wishes were granted, so during her illness, she was gifted fifteen visions, or "showings" as she called them, where she came to know the reality of Christ's passion, His pain on the cross, the blessed assurance of Divine Love. Her life of dedication proved inspirational for many women chosing a nun's life of service. She is known for the overarching ideal that "All shall be well."

Kevin of Glendalough (498-612 AD)

Kevin was an unlikely monk, a nobleman born in the royal line of the Kings of Leinster. Yet even at his birth, angelic lights surrounded the babe to alert the parents that he was special. The blackbird became his totem animal as the songbird welcomed the lad into the world. Education began at the age of seven with three different monks who commented on the serious nature of the boy and his facility for learning. After completing his studies, Kevin set off alone into the Wicklow Mountains where he stayed in the lovely valley between two lakes, Glendalough. Due to his gentle nature, Kevin was often seen in the company of animals such as otters, blackbirds, and deer. It is here that he experienced angelic visitations, the kindness of farming neighbors, and soon students who wished to learn the mysteries he uncovered through meditation. The monastic site grew, and Kevin lived in harmony with man and nature until his death at age one hundred fourteen.

Ciaran of Clonmacnoise (512-544AD)

Ciaran was a man with vision, reared in the tradesman line yet educated by his maternal grandmother: a bard, a poet, and historian. Ciaran's earliest miracle occurred when he took a cow with him as tuition to study in Clonard with St. Finian. The cow, newly mothering a calf, separated from her youngster only after Ciaran drew a line in the sand with his staff. The cow remained with Ciaran for the rest of her days, even serving him in death by the use of her hide for a psalter (book) covering. Ciaran traveled to the Aran Islands where he studied under St. Enda, learning much about healing from the holy well located there. Once completing his studies, he founded his own monastery at Clonmacnoise, later known as the first university of Ireland. Based along the banks of the River Shannon, this ideal setting housed an entire community of believers, both men and women alike. He was often likened to the character of Jesus by those who knew his gentle and giving nature. Ciaran died in his thirtieth year from the yellow plague, just as the monastery was growing, yet his vision grounded the way for many pilgrims over the years to come.

Brendan,

The

Navigator

DINGLE PENINSULA

Ogham Stone

(Druid Tree Alphabet)

Coastal View

PART ONE: THE VISION

OPENER: I, Saint Brendan of Ireland, greet you all this morning. You may know me better as Brendan the Navigator, and it is this tale of the Journey of the Soul that I bring to you now.

BEGINNING

Ship's Log: *Today we begin a most wondrous journey, that of discovering the Land of Promise, the land where those dwell who have come before us throughout our ancestry. Oh, but wouldn't Ita laugh at her young fosterling on such an undertaking! Why she would cross her arms over her chest and exclaim, "Now Bren, are you still full of thoughts traveling west? I'd be the last to say a fault against you, being like my own son you are, but seeing angels in a field of corn, pointin' west, could mean many things." Oh, how she loved the lad in me. But where else but upon the high seas of adventure could a lad find fulfillment after being reared by a saint then mentored by a Bishop? Though some call me a fool, I be no errand boy in search of lost treasure. Nay, I voyage far from home and hearth in the name of my Beloved Lord, to see His marvels, tell of his teachings, and listen to the whispers of angels.*

The night before our departure on the grandest journey of my life, I sat atop a high hill overlooking the Irish western coast on Dingle Peninsula with my sailing companions encircling me. In future years, this place would be called "Brendan's Seat." I looked upon the rolling sea, those sapphire waves of the cold Atlantic, and wondered what lay beyond those swells. Would we find the Island of the Saints, that Land of Promise? Would our boat be seaworthy enough for months, perhaps years bouncing about on those tumultuous waves with God only knows what creatures in the ocean depths beneath us? I felt fears rising for the safety of the men who followed me, faithful brothers all. As their leader, it would be up to me to remain steadfast in this mission, to follow angelic guidance, and heed my Master's voice. For this heavenly voice was directing me to the sacred seas, in search of the Land of Promise, so we could then tell others, who in turn would believe in the beauty and wonder of such a place.

One young monk leaned forward, saying, "So, it is a holy voyage we undertake then?"

"That we do, my lad," I said, now looking seaward, "if you be willing. What do you advise me, for my heart is fixed like the foot of the compass, ever onward to this blessed isle. So, shall you come with me after all, with God's help?"

"With God's help we will," they chorused.

"Then let us fast for forty days, yet no more than three at a time, in preparation for our journey."

And so we did. On the morning of our departure, we took our places in the vessel that was soon to become our home. Our boat, a wooden-ribbed curragh covered in tanned ox-hides made supple by fats, held eleven of my Clonfert monks, along with provisions for forty days, plus two additional hides for boat repairs. The curragh was also equipped with oars should the winds fade, yet a single sail masted in the center seem to say to the wind, "Guide me." As voyagers now, we steadied the oars, looked to the west, and set out.

We stopped for three days and three nights in the Aran Islands to visit with the holy father, Saint Enda, asking for his blessing on this journey. As we sat in the boat, ready for the west, he spoke words of encouragement from an ancient journey prayer:

Bless to me, O God,

The earth beneath my foot,

Bless to me, O God,

The path whereon I go;

Bless to me, O God,

The thing of my desire;

Thou Evermore of evermore,

Bless Thou to me my rest.

Bless to me the thing

Whereon is set my mind,

Bless to me the thing

Whereon is set my love;

Bless to me the thing

Whereon is set my hope;

O Thou King of Kings,

Bless Thou to me mine eye!

PART TWO: THE VOYAGE and CYCLES REVEALED

Ship's Log: *After only fifteen days, the winds have deserted us. The men seized the oars with great vigor, yet their strength is receding like the endless waves. I told them that God is our helper, our best sailor and helmsman to guide us. They thought I was crazed when I requested they bring in the oars and wait upon God, for a wind would come. Yet like many Irish brethren before us who had sail to foreign climes for Christ's sake without even oars, they knew that such faith was justified. The icy blues and cold greys of the waves filled them with fear, yet I remained steadfast. Suddenly guiding winds arose and blew us onward until the end of the forty days when our food supplies disappeared. Strengthen our faith, o Lord, and bring us into a land of your choosing.*

Island of Hospitality

Soon after this entry we landed in a place I called "The Island of Hospitality." For who should greet us first but a dog, come running right to me and sat at my feet as if I was his master. He wagged his tail then took off, glancing back at me, eager that I should follow him. "Brothers, I believe God has provided a guide for us. Come, let us see what this island holds." So we followed, and grateful we were, for he led us directly to the center of town to a great hall fully furnished: comfortable beds, chairs, and fresh water. Hanging on the walls were ornamental silver vessels, bridles, and horns. A meal was laid before us by the brethren of this isle, so we ate our fish, white bread, and water; we remained three days. Then the townspeople supplied us with enough bread and water to last us to Easter.

The Island of Sheep

The next island I called "The Island of the Sheep" for when we landed here, on Maundy Thursday, the rolling hills were littered with fluffy spots of sheep more numerous than we had ever seen. Thinking we would celebrate the Resurrection rites here, I told the monks to prepare a lamb for the feast.

We were met by a monk who told me a curious thing. He prostrated himself on the ground before me, and as I knelt beside him, he said that we were to remain only through Holy Saturday. He then pointed to the sea, saying, "See, there is the island where you will hold the nightly vigil then proceed west to another island called 'Paradise of the Birds.' There you will remain until the octave of Pentecost. Since your boat cannot carry more, I will bring you whatever food you require." Believing his leading to be from God, we set forth just as he described.

The first island for our evening stay was stark, stony with only pieces of driftwood upon it, such a contrast to the green hills we had just left. As darkness fell, a knowing came over me as to the truth of this place, but since the men were heavily into prayer, I remained inside the curragh, lest they be terrified. The next morning, as they tried to boil hot water to cook some raw meat for our meal, the island began to tremble, shake, and roll like the ocean waves. The monks leapt inside the boat, and we watched as the fire atop the island moved steadily away from us, almost for a clear two miles. I knew I must tell them the truth, for it had come to me in prayer. I said, "Brothers, be not afraid. We were not upon an island but a great fish, whose name is Jasconius, whom God has provided for our respite." Their eyes flew open wide then their fears melted into laughter. What a glorious Creator we have!

Paradise of Birds

Just as our friend had told us, we arrived soon after at a lush island with groves of trees and grasslands filled with flowers. We discovered a fresh water spring with an extraordinary tree rising about it, for the massive width matched its height. But more wondrous was that on every limb were white leaves! Yet as I looked closer, I realized they were not leaves at all but rather birds whose fluttering wings created a chorus of bells. I had never heard anything like it - and implored my God to reveal the secret of these feathered creatures, for surely there was a mystery afoot here. My prayer was answered as one of the birds spoke to me, telling her story: "We are angels who survived the Great Angelic War. Although we were not in league with Lucifer, his destruction brought about ours as well. So we travel the world in spirit form, without suffering, yet on holy days were are clothed with feathers and given voices to sing praises. You have traveled these waters for one year now, and six more lie before you where your time upon the sea will be broken down into feast day cycles: Maunday Thursday on Island of Sheep, Holy Saturday upon the back of Jasconius, Easter on Paradise of the Birds, and eight months later spend Christmas with the elders on the Island of the Community of

Ailbe. In the seventh year, you will find your heart's desire: The Land of Promise."

I cannot tell you what joy filled my heart at hearing her words. The angelic bird flew up into the trees where all her companions burst into song. Over the next day we celebrated Easter with a renewed gladness of heart.

PART THREE: RENEWABLE RESOURCES
Island of the Community of Ailbe

The steward who offered this Easter ritual returned as he promised with provisions, so we set off once more. For three months we journeyed, eating only every second or third day until we came to the Island of the Community of Ailbe. It took forty days of circling this island to find a landing place. Our strength was failing due to utter exhaustion, yet finally we spotted a narrowing with two springs: one clear, one muddy.

Immediately we were met by a man with snow-white hair whose face shone brighter than sparkling sunlight on the waves. He prostrated himself on the ground then rose and embraced me, brother to brother. He led us to the monastery where we met the other twenty-three brethren. When I questioned him, he raised his finger to his lips, reminding me of the rule of silence. The brothers spoke aloud through songs, washed our feet, and embraced each one of us in holy greeting. A bell rang as we were seated at a high table where loaves of bread were shared, one loaf per pair. I must tell you the sweetness and savory flavor of that bread is still with me!

Another bell rang, and now the abbot addressed us, telling us the patterns of this wondrous place. "My brothers, drink now in love from the clear flowing stream. We use the warm muddy waters to wash our feet. Each day the bread is supplied for us, yet who bakes this bread we do not know, although we are certain of our Lord's charity. Even today a double supply was given in anticipation of your coming. This has been our sustenance now for eighty years - for we suffer neither old age nor weakness of limbs. Heat and cold remain at bay."

"Yet how could the human flesh exist on such limits?" I asked.

The abbot replied, "It is by the mystery of Christ alone. Even our chapel lights were brought from our homeland of Ireland, yet none are reduced, for a fiery arrow flies through the window, lighting all the altars then disappears silently into the night." He led me to the candles where I saw that although they burned, no tallow slipped down the taper's side.

The abbot smiled at me, saying, "The light is spiritual, just like the light which burned before Moses yet the bush was not affected. Come, you will stay with us through Epiphany then you must be on your way once more."

PART FOUR: WONDERS

Ship's Log: *I cannot tell you that all was well those years upon the sea. Often our bodies were pushed to exhaustion. On one island God refreshed our bodies once again with grapes as big as apples. A great bird dropped a cluster of these grapes on my lap just as we were approaching the island - thanks be to God our Great Sustainer! So when we landed and saw trees covered in these delights, I also discovered six clear wells each surrounded with edible plants and roots of all kinds. I determined that this island was a place of sustenance and refreshment for our wearied bodies, so we remained here for forty days. As we left this place, we took as much fruit as the boat could bear.*

Our faith was sorely tested, despite the miracles we partook of with other brothers. Why once we saw a beast rise like a tower before us, ready to devour us. His massive body caused the waves to erupt about him, causing us to use the oars to steady ourselves. I cried out, "Lord, deliver your servants, as you did Jonah from the belly of the whale." Our God was quick to reply, for suddenly a second monster, breathing fire from its maw, splintered the waves before us. "Brothers, this battle will not harm us, but see now the glory of God." And so we did as this monster from the west attacked the beast, slaying it right before our eyes.

The Crystal Pillar

The marvelous creatures we encountered were truly wondrous, yet I believe the most mystifying thing was the Crystal Pillar. We had sailed further north than ever before, having been on this journey for several years now, miraculously finding our way back to the islands foretold to celebrate the holy feast days each year. I spotted the pillar first, rising out of the waves like a four-sided castle tower yet sparkling as if made of silver, and so high it reached into the sky! As we moved closer, I saw a wide-meshed net surrounding the base with openings so big our curragh could safely pass through. We took down the sail and gently rowed into this sacred space.

I was so curious about this massive pillar that we rode the circumference, which I measured to be approximately seven hundred yards on each side. Then, on the fourth day, we found a chalice and paten (the thin metal plate for Eucharist) made of the same crystal as the pillar and the net. I took these two objects, raising them high and said, "Our Lord has shown us this wonder, and provided these two Eucharistic vessels as proof so that others may believe." We then held the divine service and refreshed our bodies, for we had remained in such awe of this pillar that we had not taken food for four days. As we passed again through the mesh to leave, we raised a sail which billowed and blossomed before us for the next eight days, allowing us rest.

Island of Smiths

The most frightening isle we encountered was barren of trees or vegetation yet filled with rocks, smiths' forges, and slag, remnants of burning ores. I sensed a deep unease about this place and wondered why the wind had brought us here. "My brothers, we will not stop nor go nearer to this place," I exclaimed, making the sign of the cross. The thundering sound of bellows and hammers striking anvils assailed our senses. As we were turning the boat, I spotted a shaggy man full of darkness and fire. He reached his tongs into the red-hot coals, and grasping a lump of burning slag, slung it towards us with all his might. It missed the boat, but the sea responded in sizzling smoke. The smith was soon joined by others, each one flinging hot lumps over our heads. The island looked like one huge furnace with a sulfuric stench that now filled the air. The tranquil sea transformed into a bubbling, boiling soup pot. Once we were away, I felt as if we had glimpsed the depths of Hell itself.

Land of Promise

Having traveled for five years, and seen many wonders, my heart was still heavy since we had not found the Land of Promise. We returned briefly to Ireland, where my foster mother Ita told me that to find this place, I must rebuild the boat entirely of wood then set upon the breast of the sea once more. And so we did.

The cycles of feast days resumed, and at the end of two years we landed once again at the Paradise of Birds for the Easter celebrations. The steward whom we met the first year came to me, saying, "This time I will be your guide, for without me you will not find the Land of Promise." My heart sang within me - finally our true destination lay just before us. We loaded provisions for forty days, and as we set sail, the angelic birds rose up in songs of praise.

At the end of the forty days, a great mist enveloped the boat, so dense that we could not see the man seated beside us. The steward asked me if I knew this fog's origin, and when I answered no, he said, "This fog encircles the island for which you've searched many long years." My heart leapt for joy within me, yet the island itself remained a mystery for another hour until a bright light embraced it, causing the misty curtain to melt away.

We moored the boat and began to walk on this wondrous shore full of ripe fruit trees and fresh water wells. The ground was littered with precious gems, gleaming in deep maroons, royal purples, sapphire blues, and flaming ambers. We meandered through its woods for forty days, feasting off salmon and honey, and still could not find the end of it. Rather, we saw the great river which divided the island.

On the other side of the river, we were hailed by a shining youth, who greeted us in holy earnest. He spoke to me, saying, "Saint Brendan, here is the Land of Promise which you have sought now for seven years. God did not bring you here immediately, for He wanted you to know the wonders of the great sea. As proof of its existence, take as much of the gems and fruit your vessel will hold. This land remains as you see it, with neither shadow nor night, for its light is Christ." I pondered this, thinking truly this was a mystery yet to be revealed.

We took our leave of this angel, loaded the boat, and sailed south, our hearts at peace. We could return from our pilgrimage with tales of wonder, ponderous sights, and spiritual mysteries that would take generations to unravel. Although our tales may be told in future generations as a blending of folklore and truth, know this: we did sail, we did travel, and we did cross the veil.

CLOSING

I close with these words for all journeymen:

Though your destination is not yet clear

You can trust the promise of its opening;

Unfurl yourself into the grace of beginning

That is at one with your life's desire.

AMEN

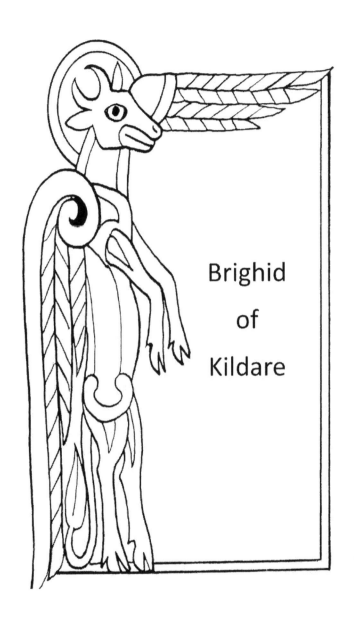

Brighid

of

Kildare

KILDARE

Brighid's Flame Memorial

Brighid's Fire Pit

BRIGHID OF KILDARE MONOLOGUE

OPENER:

Bless, O God, my little cow

Bless, O God, my desire;

Bless Thou my partnership

And the milking of my hands.

Give the milk, my treasure!

Give the milk my treasure,

Give quietly, with steady flow,

Give the milk, my treasure!

With steady flow and calmly.

In the name of my risen Lord, I greet you this day as Saint Brighid, a woman by many names. In my homeland of Ireland, they simply called me "Brigit" while the Scots named me Bride, the Welsh named me San Ffraid, and the British named me Brigantia. They even call me "Mary of the Gaels." I come whenever called, regardless of the translation.

PART ONE: EARLY DAYS

For those of you who are unfamiliar with my life, my deeds on this earth in service to my dear Christ, let me now share a few of those details with you in the hopes of flaming a fire in your own heart. It all began with a prophecy.

You see, my mother Broetsech was a bondswoman, a milking maid within the household of a nobleman named Dubhthach. Despite his marriage, he loved her to the point of conceiving me. Now one day, when they were out riding in the cart, they passed a druid who stopped them. My mother was heavy in the belly by that time, but as the Druid cast his eyes over her, he told Dubhthach this woman would bear a girl who would be great, a "daughter whose radiance shall outshine the sun." Don't you know that made the man swell with pride! But when his wife heard of this, she demanded my mother be sold, immediately.

So she was, to a poet, yet Dubhthach still claimed me since he saw possible riches in his future for so rare a daughter.

Well, wouldn't you know another Druid came to visit that poet, and when he saw my mother sitting in the chair, he had a vision of a great pillar of flame shining just above her belly. Nobody else saw it, but this Druid knew the importance of such a vision, so he bought my mother straight away. By now, she was almost at my birthing time, and not long afterwards as she was returning from her milking chores, the birth pangs came upon her. I was born right on the threshold, neither within nor without. Later, some folks say that my coming into this world was a blending of the old ways and new beliefs. The other servants took the two of us inside, bathed me in fresh milk then took care of us both. But even as a wee babe, I could not keep down me mother's milk, so the Druid brought home a special cow, a white one with red ears. Now some folks say that be an animal of the Good People, the Fey, but whether that be true or not, I took pleasure in its gift and thrived, growing into a healthy child. That's why in Scotland they sometimes call me the "Milkmaid Bride" or "Golden-Haired Bride of the Kine."

It seems that I did give the neighbors a scare though. Once, while sleeping in my cradle, the neighbors thought our house was on fire. They rushed in to find me sleeping, and not a flame about except over my head, lightly dancing as if over embers. The Druid told them not to worry, for I kindled a fire within me. Twas him that named me, for he had a dream (and you know Druids believe greatly in the power of dreams) of three shining figures (angels I believe) who told him to baptize me "Sancta Brigida" (Brighid) meaning "fiery arrow." And so it was. Why, when I reached the marrying age and Dubhthach tried to sell me off as bride, I confess that a raging fire burned within me, and I vowed to pluck out me own eyes, for I would never be a wife.

PART TWO: BLENDING BELIEFS

The Druid taught me well in ways of learning through reading, meditation, and long walks in the woods. He reminded me constantly of our ever-growing bond to nature and the invaluable lessons held in its mysteries. As Christianity spread, the Old Ways were often absorbed into new ways of viewing the spirit. Without turning my back on my childhood beliefs, I felt the call within my soul to serve this man Jesus, this risen Christ, so I took the veil of Christianity at the tender age of twenty-two. Even during the ceremony, the flames of my life persisted, for those present say they saw a column of flame engulf me while Bishop Mel read me the rites. Perhaps that is why he became confused and rather than enjoining me as a nun, he read the passages for a Bishop. When this error was pointed out, he declared that the act was done, and it must have been in accordance with God's higher order for me. So, as the rites were upheld, I became the youngest abbess ever.

The rites of the Old Ways and the mysteries of Christ blended in harmony within me. You see, I never saw either practice exclusive of the other, and maintained that belief throughout all my years of service. Many others believed that two such views of a spiritual life could exist side by side with parallel approaches to spirituality, a merging of the older traditions with the new faith known as Celtic Christianity.

I searched for a place where I could minister to others, create a community where men and women in monastic service could live and worship together, sharing a commonality of all beliefs. While searching, I came upon some land in Kildare owned by a local king. When I approached him about this land, this miserly man laughed saying, "I'll give you as much land as your mantle about your shoulders will cover." Wearing a confident smile, he looked around at his men who nodded in agreement. So, with the mysteries of Christ in my heart, I laid the cloak upon the ground and began to pray. To everyone's astonishment, myself included, the mantle began to grow. It spread wider and wider, covering hills and valleys, streams, and rocks until the proud man begged me to make it cease. His men said I was no saint but the goddess Brigit herself, and this act was a reminder of when she had spread her mantle as a protective covering for all of Erin.

And so a monastery was founded, in Cell-Dara or Kildare, meaning "the church of the oak." I was pleased to discover that patrons of the goddess Brigit had worshipped here, in the sacred oak grove, where the goddess kept alive an eternal flame, some say for centuries. And so, we too, lit a flame saying, "May this light burn forever in the world and may it never go out." Twenty nuns rotated a watch, and I hope they will continue to burn this blaze for years far beyond my own. I felt such a kinship to this ancient Brigit - through name, through flame. For I am the fire. I am the dancing flame. I am the heart of the ember. I burn with the love of my Lord. Like the goddess before me, I became known as the patron of smithcraft, poetry, and the hearth. So I, too, in years to come, would have believers continue this tradition in my name while tending their home fires:

Brigit, excellent woman,

Flame golden, sparkling,

May she bear us to the eternal kingdom,

She the sun, fiery, radiant!

Smooring the fire (*covering embers with peat at night*) with this ancient invocation:

I will smoor the hearth

As Brighid the foster-mother would smoor

The Foster-mother's holy name

Be on the hearth, be on the herd, be on the household all."

Those who came within our walls were well-schooled in arts and letters, Biblical knowledge, and the artistry of illumination. We created a Book of Kildare, an artful presentation of our Lord's life here on earth as revealed through the four gospels. The margins were filled with colorful creatures in gentle twists and turns for the inclusion of all nature amidst never-ending knots to symbolize eternity. What a celebration for our Master's brushwork of the imagination! I always felt close to my God when I viewed Him as the Great Creator, praising the colorful diversity within all nature. Perhaps my early training in the household of a Druid allowed me to view the world in layers, a continuity of all that has come before with all that is to come.

PART THREE: LEGENDS and HEALINGS

The Lord touched my life at an early age in the ways of increase. I thought it was magic at the time, but these events later came to be known as miracles. Once while visiting my father Dubhthach, he asked me to prepare a meal for one of his noble guests. I was given 5 strips of bacon (quite a treat), yet when the bacon was done, I found the man asleep by the fire. I looked about wondering what to do when a poor, hungry dog came into the house. I slipped him one piece, and then another. Unbeknownst to me the guest awoke and saw me handing over his meal to the dog. Yet when Dubhthach asked me how many strips of bacon were in the pan, I counted five. Imagine! I saw this happen time and again, with butter, milk, sheep, cattle, even pigs! Whatever number was present at the first, it often doubled in my presence. Why even at Kildare we once had an unexpected visit from seven bishops. We'd already milked the cows three times that day and consumed all that had been graciously given, yet an angel told me to milk them again. And so I did. So much milk flowed that it overflowed the Leinster fields and created "The Lake of Milk."

As abbess, I was often called upon for healing the sick, and this I did with a gladness of heart. They all came: blind, lepers, dumb, consumptives, even lunatics. I praise the Master Healer for working through me. Some said that even touching my shadow would make them whole again. For me, one of the most distressing times came early in my life. Once again, my father learned of these amazing feats and fetched me back to Leinster with my nurse. She fell ill on the journey. We stopped at a lord's home where feasting was in its height, and that selfish man would naught even give us water much less a cup of his precious ale. We turned from the house, but soon came upon a well. I recited these ancient words of healing over it:

From Thee all skill and science flow,

All pity, care, and love.

All calm and courage, faith and hope;

O pour them from above.

Then, in drawing up the bucket, I gave my nurse some rich, cool ale. I later heard that the lord's own barrels mysteriously ran dry.

Yet for myself, in later years, I became ill with headaches so intense paired with blurred vision that I could hardly stand. Bishop Mel sent me to a famous healer, yet on the way, I was overcome with a dizzy spell and fell right off the horse. I'm told I struck my head upon a stone and began to bleed profusely. My companions and I reached the Healer, but he confessed he could do nothing for me since there was no greater source than myself. Yet once these words were spoken aloud, I felt the strength returning to my body, all bleeding ceased. I was suddenly healthy once more and discovered a new gift, that of "inner world sight" where my spiritual intuitions about people and their situations were clarified. So when those with illness came to me, this new intuition allowed me to work more specifically and effectively.

Despite the honor and respect often given to me following a healing incident, I learned that the true motivation for the "miracle" came from the compassion in my heart. When I heard of injustices, that fiery nature of mine was set aflame once more, and I was able to free men from their chains, open closed doors, even provide a tame fox where a servant was wrongfully imprisoned after killing a king's favorite pet. Once, another king's servant accidentally broke a precious cup, so that regal threw the man in prison - for a broken cup! I was outraged. I asked for the shards, placed them in my hand and breathed upon them. I held up the restored cup for all to see saying, "See how the life of a soul, though it be broken, may yet be made whole."

Yet what many of those in Ireland know me for is as the Foster Mother of Christ, the mid-wife in the barn with the Blessed Mary in her time of need. I was awakened in the middle of the night by two angels at my bedside. They covered me with their wings and transported me through the ripples of time to assist in the birth of Jesus. You can imagine my astonishment at finding myself in a barn with the blessed couple! The animals quieted as Mary held Joseph's hand so tightly that the poor man could naught move a muscle. The birth pangs were deeply upon her, and though she did not scream, the strength of the contractions lined her face. I drew water from the animal trough, checked the small fire, and grabbing the saddle blanket, stayed by her side until the wee lad came into the night. The three of us were exhausted yet filled with a happiness beyond words, for we knew in a moment He was the Son of God, sung into the world by a heavenly chorus of angels:

Come Thou long expected Jesus, born to set thy people

free;

From our fears and sins release; let us find our rest in Thee.

Israel's strength and consolation, Hope of all the earth Thou art

Dear Desire of every nation, joy of every longing heart.

Born thy people to deliver, born a child and yet a King;

Born to reign in us forever, now thy gracious kingdom bring.

By Thine own eternal Spirit rule in all our hearts alone;

By Thine own sufficient merit raise us to Thy glorious throne.

PART FOUR: SOUL FRIEND

So if you think on my life, some would say I am known for the mystery of increase, compassion for the poor, patron saint for midwives and healers while maintaining a continuity of belief between the Ancient ways and the lessons of Christ. As we walk in life, I encouraged the men and women of Kildare to find an "anam cara" (soul friend), someone who holds you in profound recognition, a spiritual bond that exceeds this earthly realm. This friend honors the secrets of your heart, extending hospitality through acceptance of your deepest thoughts and aspirations while nudging your dreams into being.

I tried to instill in everyone I met that true miracles come from an open heart and generous spirit, cloaked in patience, honored in the solitudes of prayer.

CLOSING: So it is I wish for you all to know how to increase the bounty of your spiritual life through personal acts of compassion and generosity. To discover what kind of fire illuminates your life, you simply need to recall the Source of All Love and Imagination.

On the night of Jesus's birth, I said a blessing , so please stand and repeat after me:

The sacred Three

To save, To shield, To surround

The hearth, The house, The household,

This eve, This night,

Oh, this eve, This night, and every night,

Each single night.

Amen.

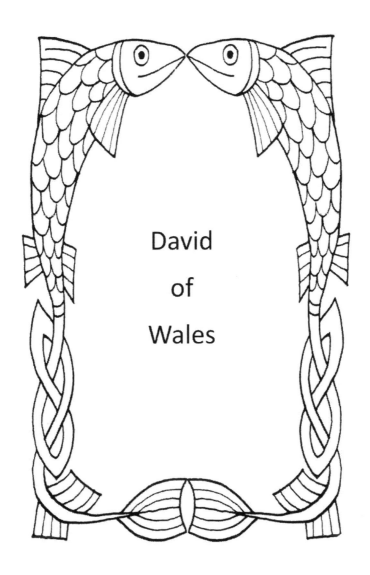

David

of

Wales

Saint David's Sea and Sky

DAVID OF WALES MONOLOGUE

OPENER: I ask that God grant you peace upon this holy day as I stand before you as Saint David or Dewi as my friends would call me. My life shows a simple way of living, a simple way of communing with fellow believers, and the simple call of Christ to serve and love others. So, this day, I will share with you some of my experiences which may in turn fuel kindness in your own hearts.

PART ONE: CHILDHOOD YEARS

I believe that writers in the days following my own might call me "the Waterman." While it is true that this holy element appeared influential during my birth upon this earth, the sanctity of water stayed strong within me throughout my life. You see, my mother Non lived alone in a cave by the sea while I grew hale and strong within her womb. She breathed in that salt air daily, strengthening my body while my soul heard the waves, their rhythmic rolls upon the strand acting as nature's lullaby. Womb and waters met earth and sea, binding me in an inexplicable depth that followed me all my days.

One day my mother told me of my birth. When the time came for delivery, she was alone save God and his elements. Great peals of thunder shook the clouds as wild winds drove the frothing waves to ground. Slashes of light split the sky as she screamed with the birth pains, bringing me into this world in a flash of brilliancy. The storm abated, and I was free now to find God on my own in years to come. She felt the miracle of life and wanted me to know God's greatness. She often stood in the water while holding me close to her chest, close to her heart, saying this prayer:

The little wavelet for thy form,

The little wavelet for thy voice,

The little wavelet for thy sweet speech.

The little wavelet for thy means,

The little wavelet for thy generosity,

The little wavelet for thine appetite.

The little wavelet for thy wealth,

The little wavelet for thy life,

The little wavelet for thine health.

Nine waves of grace to thee,

The waves of the Physician of thy salvation.

In my early years we were taken to a palace where I was told my father lived, King Sandde of Ceredigion. As I grew, the servants often whispered as I passed, leaving me shy and alone. Finally, a kitchen maid told me the tale that sprang from their gossiping lips.

Before my birth, the king had a vision telling him to hunt then leave the spoils at a monastery for his future son. The vision was specific: a stag, a salmon, and a beehive. Fearful of not obeying, the king rode until he had completed the task. The preserved meat of the salmon and stag, along with the beehive, were transported to the monastery of Maucannus where these three gifts were held in store for his future son. While riding home along the seacoast rode, he came upon my mother Non, a young unspoiled woman at the time and took her against her will. It is from that unholy act that I came into being.

Tears sprang to my eyes as the young serving girl slipped away. Where was the glory of God my mother had spoken to me? Where was the grandeur of nature erupting on the earth in celebration of my deliverance to this life? The shame of my conception was more than my young heart could bear.

It was only years later, as a man of God, I saw how out of darkness God brought a great light of hope for both my mother and me. Is it any wonder that Non devoted her life to God, in holy service, and experienced miraculous healings for expectant mothers? This gift of healing passed through her hands and heart into those whose lives she touched.

As a lad, I still pondered the meaning behind the King's vision. I wondered about those three specific creatures being called from nature to herald my beginnings. According to ancient Celtic customs, these sacred beings inspire man through their natural ways. The bees teach us community and celebration. They know the truths of prophecy and are often regarded as guardians of the land's bounty. The Stag holds the mysteries of the forest in its untamed beauty and power. Many see him as the King of the Woods while The White Stag invites believers into imagined realms. Then the salmon, the fish from which ancient tales describe worldly wisdom. From that time to this, the salmon is still said to grant wisdom to those who partake of its flesh. Mysteries of nature - how can we know their true value except through the One who made them, the Great Creator? These animals remind me of an ancient hymn concerning the holiness of all nature:

All creatures of our God and King,

Lift up your voice with us and sing Allelluia! Allelluia!

Thou burning sun with golden beam

Thou silver moon with softer gleam, O praise Him!

Such questions swirled in my young mind until my parents fostered me into the care of Paulinus in Menevia where I stayed ten years. Here I learned to read, write, and ponder the spiritual mysteries of our day. A dove befriended me, sat upon my shoulder, and by some miracle, I could understand his speech. He would often sing to me and tell me tales about faraway lands. Perhaps my natural shyness with people allowed this winged creature and I to form a bond. I learned not to question such things. Before leaving this company, I took the vows to serve God faithfully all of my days.

My mother was not the only one to experience the gift of healing. While living with my teacher Paulinus, I discovered that he he had an engorged inflammation of the eyes. He asked other students to lay hands on him, yet nothing happened. When I approached, in order to see the damage, I knew I had to look my teacher in the face. I had never done this, always looking down in an act of reverence, though truth be told I was too shy and often felt undeserving of being in this great man's presence. So Paulinus spoke to me in faith, saying, "Without looking, place your hands upon my eyes, and I will be healed." I did as he requested, and God granted our boon, for Paulinus was immediately healed. It was then that he encouraged me to find a place of ministry.

As I wondered which path God might lay before me, we had a visitor, an elder from the Maucannus monastery. He described a dream concerning the previous actions taken by the King which had led to my birth. Paulinus believed that I should follow this elder home, so I did. As we reached the monastery, I was given the three gifts held in trust for me, the King's son. I cooked both the salmon and the stag meat then served them dripping in honey. We opened the doors to the locals - what a feast! I brought the beehive back to Menevia where I learned the husbandry of bees. This gift, like the water, stayed with me throughout my life.

PART TWO: PILGRIMAGE

Finding a Monastery

After leaving my teacher Paulinus, I traveled for quite some time throughout Wales and Britain, establishing 12 monasteries of learning and service, beginning in Glastonbury and Bath. In Bath, once again water called to me. The bathing waters had been fouled, so I blessed them and endowed them with continuous heat for healing aching bodies. Yet something kept calling me home, so I settled in the valley of Glyn Rhoslyn on the Pembrokeshire coast. I had heard that St. Patrick himself had considered this valley, yet through angelic intervention he was told that this space was reserved for another. Imagine my surprise that the Lord intended it for me!

However, I ran into a spot of trouble in setting boundaries, for the land belonged to a man named Boia whose wife insisted that we monks be driven out. Boia gave us permission as long as we created specific lines. We later learned how truly enraged his wife became, for in her jealousy and greed, she devised a wicked plan. Believing a heinous act would drive monks away, she invited her stepdaughter Dunawd to visit. The angry wife, while out supposedly gathering hazelnuts, slit the poor girl's throat, causing her blood to flow into a nearby stream. The wife then cut off the dead girl's hair as an offering to pagan gods. So ashamed was this wife or her horrendous deed that she ran away, never to be seen again. Making matters worse, pirates attacked the husband's fort and killed everyone.

I cannot begin to describe the distress I felt about these incidents. I sought out the place of Dunawd's murder, blessed the earth, and a clear spring arose, known afterwards for its healing properties. But we moved past this early disaster to form a healthy community of brothers, one in which I taught them to be mindful through small daily acts of kindness. All goods were kept in common, so to stay meant forsaking all worldly wealth; there were no "my things" once you passed into the monastic hold. We tended to our neighbors' needs and tried to live in an attitude of gratefulness for all we were given.

Daily Community Life

Our maxim was this: "Simple food, simple words, simple truths." I called my brothers into practices of silent mediation and quality prayer. We ate simple meals of fish, vegetables, bread, and herbs. Though some monasteries brewed ale, we drank only water. We were self-sufficient, conducting daily chores such as plowing, harvesting, milling flour, and fishing in the nearby river. When visitors came, enough food was always available. We served the sick, poor, widows, wards, feeble, and fellow pilgrims as we discovered the joy in service spoken of in Matthew's parable describing that as you "did it unto the least of these my brethren, you have done it unto me." For God's natural order in community is mutual support.

Give us, O God, of the morning meal

Benefit to the body, the frame of the soul;

Give us, O God, of the seventh bread,

Enough for our need at evening close.

PART THREE: WORSHIP AND MIRACLES

Daily Worship

In our daily life we adhered to the new Benedictine Rule in observance of canonical times of mediation/prayer throughout the day such as I directed for my other monasteries. Bells were rung to sound the next order of the day. After chores, we returned to our cells for reading, meditation, prayer, and writing. For Evensong we gathered in silence and chanted the psalms to uplift our souls, followed by this evening hymn:

Day is dying in the west; heaven is touching earth with rest

Wait and worship while the night

Sets her evening lamps through all the sky.

When forever from our sight pass the stars, the day, the
night

Lord of angels, on our eyes

Let eternal morning rise and shadows end.

I found the holy element of water following me deeper into my ministry. I discovered that by using a divining rod, I could aid farmers in locating underground water sources for their fields. Another incident occurred when I attended a baptism by Bishop Ailbe. Following that ritual, I blessed the waters. Immediately a clear new spring arose whose waters immediately healed a blind man. As my body remained one with water, I was often observed meditating in the sea. I would immerse myself in its restorative power, standing in depths up to my neck. I realize this life was not for everyone, and some fellow believers even considered me quite austere, but my fellow monks and I discovered a depth of joy in this singleness of devotion.

Miracles

To be recognized as a saint, one must add miracles to their life experiences. Like many saints of my day, we spoke daily with angels, sought out God's intervention then became vessels for His mighty works. One such incident happened following a visit from my friend, Saint Findbarr. We engaged in such enlightening conversations from angelic inspiration to the names of the stars that I found myself a bit bereaved at his leaving. He was traveling by boat back to Ireland, yet the strong winds delayed his passage. When he asked me if he could borrow my horse, I immediately replied, "Yes, and take him with my blessing." Well, to everyone's astonishment, the horse literally began to ride the waves with the saint on his back as if the ocean were a level plain. Findbarr later told us that he passed Saint Brendan upon his quest for the Blessed Isle. The saint rode on the back of the whale Jasconius, and both men claimed these were wondrous times. Findbarr rode all the way back to Ireland, caring for the horse until its death. This tale reminded many of the legendary Welsh figure Manannan Mac Lir, god of the sea, with a horse called Aenbarr.

Another remarkable incident involved my bees. You remember how I brought a hive with me which my father the King had first discovered. Well, these same bees were extremely plentiful, and I learned how to care for the bees and harvest their honey. Even their humming sound suited monastic life for it is lulling, like chanting. Some of the monks even likened our community to a beehive and the wisdom from my teachings as sweet as honey. So, when St. Domnoc visited us, he was so taken by the bees that he became a beekeeper, working the hives daily. When it was time for him to return to Ireland, some of the bees swarmed his ship and followed him. Supposedly this was the beginning of honey introduced into Irish monastic life. By being at one with the natural world, we live better in community, often reciting blessings and singing hymns in adoration of all brotherhood:

At length there dawns the glorious day by prophets

foretold;

At length the chorus clearer grows that shepherds heard of old.

The day of dawning brotherhood breaks on our eager eyes,

And human hatreds flee before the radiant eastern skies.

One common faith unites us all, we seek one common goal,

One tender comfort broods upon the struggling human soul.

To this clear call of brotherhood our hearts responsive ring;

We join the glorious new crusade of our great Lord and King.

I did make one more pilgrimage, this time to the Holy Land itself. And through examining my life, it was there I was granted the honor of being confirmed as archbishop then later as abbot. I believe someday I may even by known as the Patron Saint of Wales.

PART FOUR: DAVID'S PASSING

As years flew by, I was nearing the end of my days. By God's grace, I was given knowledge by the Shining Ones that my time approached. As the word spread, many visitors arrived for my last mass. I shared this humble wisdom with them, saying,

"Lords, brothers, sisters, be happy and keep your faith and your belief; and do these little things that you have heard and seen me do."

CLOSING:

I close this our time together, and hope that some piece of my life may add wisdom to your own soul peace as I leave you with this prayer:

In name of the Holy Spirit of grace,

In name of the Father of the City of peace,

In name of Jesus who took death off us,

Oh! In name of the Three who shield us in every need.

If well thou has found us tonight,

Seven times better mayest thou leave us without harm,

Thou bright white Moon of the seasons!

Amen.

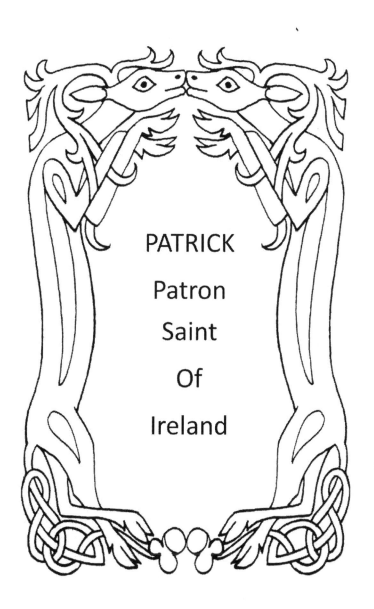

PATRICK

Patron

Saint

Of

Ireland

St. Patrick's Legacy

Pilgrim's Path

Dublin's St. Patrick's Cathedral

SAINT PATRICK MONOLOGUE

OPENER

I stand before you today a simple man, Patrick by name, one who lives only due to the grace of God. Though you may have heard bits about my life, some true, some lingering in legend, I will not boast of my deeds, but rather give a solid account for the furthering of my Lord's greatness. For He is most worthy, and I, being just a country lad, bow in all humility to my most gracious King and answer His call to bring light to the darkness.

I am bending my knee

In the eye of the Father who created me,

In the eye of the Son who purchased me,

In the eye of the Spirit who cleansed me,

In friendship and affection.

EARLY LIFE and PROPHECIES

My life in Dumbarton, Scotland, began with a miracle. When I was young, my father Calpurnius once told me this tale. He said my mother, Concess, while pregnant with me, was washing the feet of a local king who harbored dark and lustful thoughts towards her. The king's jealous wife put poison in my mother's drink, yet for some unknown reason the poison did not affect her. Soon afterwards, I was born, holding a stone in my hand. My father Calpurnius declared that I had hardened the poison, holding it firm in my fist to save my mother. There it seems my life of righting injustices began.

The second miracle, relayed to me by my mother, occurred during my baptism. As a babe, I was taken to a blind priest, Gornias, for his blessing. He lived in a dark cave, and my mother walked bravely to his home. As he placed his hand upon my head, he said, "His name shall be Patrick. He will outreach all others in this land. His name shall be remembered throughout Ireland and beyond." As he lifted his hand from my head, he blinked his eyes several times then burst into tears, claiming his sight had been restored. My mother thanked Gornias for this astonishing blessing.

The men in my family were educated Christians: my grandfather Potitus as a priest and my father as an ordained deacon. The scriptures were read aloud to me throughout my youth. But being just a child, I let the words in yet did not own them until much later. However, I do recall two incidents during the time I was fostered to my mother's sister that made me wonder about the power of prayer.

Both events dealt with the elements of water and fire. The first happened during a dreadful winter storm with winds so strong they shook my foster mother's walls, crept through the cracks, and put out the fire. I wailed, "How shall we eat without fire?" But suddenly an idea came to me. I took dry straw and laid it like logs in the hearth. Then I dipped my hand into water, raced to the straw, and allowed the drops to fall on it, praying for fire. As each droplet fell, they transformed into sparks. The straw blazed, so I fed the fire with small bits of wood until a fire flickered to life. All was well. You can imagine her surprise!

The second event happened when I was asked to gather wood for the fire. But it was so cold, all I came back with were icicles. My foster mother was furious, saying "These will not warm us!" But once again I prayed, saying, "If only we believe, these icicles will blaze brighter than wood!" Then I flung the icicles into the hearth, and they flared up into brilliant flames. I sat back in wonder at how the elements of both water and fire heard my voice.

Well, now my foster mother was full of suspicions. She decided to test me, not once, but twice. The first time she was bemoaning how all the other children brought fresh honey to their mothers, yet I never gave her such a gift. I took up a crockery of water, blessed it, and handed it to her. She looked inside, smiled, then placed her fingers in the jar and pulled out the most amazing honey she'd ever tasted. I received a grand hug for that gift, I can tell you!

The second test, however, took me quite by surprise. I was taken down to the milking sheds, but quite unknown to me, a neighbor's son had died in the night. My foster mother requested that the lad be brought to the milking sheds then laid in the straw. I did not see him at first, being rather busy with the task of milking. After I drank my share from the foaming jug, she said to me, "Patrick, call that other boy to share the milk." So I did, saying, "Boy, come share my drink." The dead child awoke, rose, and drank. The two women were utterly amazed while I considered that the prophecies of Gornias about me were beginning to come true.

Temper my spirit, O Lord

Keep it long in the fire;

Make it one with the flame,

Let it share That upreaching desire.

IRISH SLAVERY and ESCAPE

I remained in fosterage for many years, schooling with local children and learning a farmer's life. When I turned sixteen, while visiting family in Wales, my sister Lupait and I were kidnaped by angry Irish raiders where my life as a freeman was brutally exchanged for a life of servitude. We were given to a man named Miliuc, King of Dalraida, on the northern coast. My sister served in the household while I spent six long years under harsh conditions tending sheep. The coastal winds tore at my thin clothing while I watched over my wooly charges. How many times I'd wished I could exchange my cloak for their fine wool coats! The Fochlad Woods, dense and dark, were bordered by grazing lands where I spent my days while nighttime brought ferocious cries and feral yellow eyes. It was through God's power and words alone that I was safe.

> Thou, my soul's Healer
>
> Keep me at even
>
> Keep me at morning,
>
> Keep me at noon
>
> Help and safeguard
>
> My means this night.

I once again learned the power of prayer, speaking freely to my God daily, often a hundred times, in snow, ice, and rain. I came to the know the voice of a ministering angel, Victoricus, who comforted me and encouraged me with his words. He taught me about the deeper levels of the spirit, pushing me to uncover the secret places of my soul. It was during my slavery that my early training in the Scriptures came to life, burning a fire in my spirit. I began sharing these lessons with fellow workers, having learned some of their native tongue, who in turn shared these truths with others as many came to know the wonders of Christ.

I prayed often for release from my captivity, and at the end of six years, Victoricus told me that it was time for me to return to my homeland, for a ship was waiting for me. In order to gain my freedom, I was instructed to follow a boar into the woods. I heeded the angel's words, watching the boar with his mighty tusks tear into the earth. He abandoned the hole, and after he left, I dug a bit deeper still. Imagine my wonder when I unearthed two gold pieces, enough to purchase not only my own freedom but Lupait's as well. The location of the ship was over two hundred miles south along the coast. Quickly gathering supplies, we made a hasty retreat and began our journey home.

At last, we came upon the coastal village of Wexford and there saw the boat prepared for our safe passage. At first the captain was distrustful of me, a Breton, and refused my plea for room upon his ship. But after much prayer, I was recalled to this ship and told to come aboard. My sister and I traveled across fitful seas for three days. Once we reached land, she journeyed north to return to our family while I traveled for twenty-eight days south into the wilderness with some of the pagan lads. Our food supplies quickly ran out, and a great hunger fell upon the entire group. Their angry cries set me on edge, still hoping somehow to bring them into the faith. I begged them, "Turn in faith with all your hearts to the Lord my God because nothing is impossible for Him so that He may put food in your way - enough to be fully satisfied." *[Translated quote from St. Patrick's Confessio]*. No sooner had the words escaped my lips than a herd of pigs suddenly appeared! We ate our fill, remaining for two days until our health was restored before moving on. Great is our God who supplies all our needs!

MONASTIC STUDIES

I left the lads, ready to seek my new spiritual path under the guidance once again of Victoricus. I was able to study in Gaul under the fine teachings of Bishop Germanus in Auxerre. It was here that I continued to learn every benefit of the soul: gaining wisdom, knowledge, and purity enveloped in a great fear and love of God. I wished only to serve in goodness with singleness of heart. My studies were interrupted by the sudden death of Palladius, a missionary in Ireland. The thought of returning to Ireland, now a freeman once again, filled me with both confusion and conviction. It wasn't until Victoricus told me in a dream that Ireland cried out specifically for me that my heart softened. He showed me multitudes of letters with sincere voices begging my return. One voice stood out among the many, saying, "We beg you, holy boy, to come and walk again among us." *[Translated quote from St. Patrick's Confessio]*. I awoke with renewed courage and accepted the post once my ordination vows were completed. In the years to come, I was ordained as deacon, priest, and finally bishop.

RETURN TO IRELAND

I sailed north, back towards the lands of my enslavement.
It was there my faith was renewed, so it was there my ministry
would begin. I prayed over the waves as we neared my new
home.

Relieve Thou, O God, each one

In suffering on land or sea,

In grief or wounded or weeping,

And lead them to the house

Of Thy peace this night.

May Brighid shield me,

May Mary shield me,

May Michael shield me,

On sea and on land.

Just prior to landing, we came upon a small island where I was met by a man and woman well beyond age. They had been charged to wait for a specific monk before leaving that home. "I am that man," I said, having confirmed their situation with Victoricus. The grateful couple, now free to leave, offered me an unusual gift: a staff with intricate designs. "Take this. Let it be your sign, and with it you carry our blessings," said the husband. I held the staff in my hands and knew that in years to come this "holy staff" would remain with me, a powerful image of God's righteousness.

We soon landed in Northern Ireland in County Down, and with my staff in hand, I began teaching the locals, speaking to them in their native tongue. My first church was established following the conversion of a local chief, Dichu, who offered his barn as a place of worship. This would be the first of many churches, many converts. Who would have ever foretold the misery of slavery would blossom into such fruit!

MIRACLES and ROYAL CONFRONTATIONS

As the Lord instructed his servants to become "fishers of men," so I felt this call burning in my breast as I set upon bringing the Irish people into the light of Christ. Rather than follow in the footsteps of my fellow brethren by establishing monastic sites, my focus became the heart of the individual. By my speaking in their native tongue, the Irish people came to trust me, listen to me, and soon found their hearts turn from the old superstitions to follow the One True God.

My ways were not always gentle, and at times, I know my teachings offended even my superiors, yet God's grace led me forward. I spent years in the northern climes, slowly moving westward towards Galway. It was in this region that I walked up a mighty hill once with a specific purpose in mind. Upon this height I spent forty days in the wilderness, in remembrance of my Lord, and like Him, was tempted and tormented. Victoricus remained with me, speaking with me daily, bringing me encouragement during my fasting and prayers. Writhing lizards like snakes fell upon me, so I banished them from all of Ireland. Yea, even a mighty cluster of blackbirds as thick as clouds descended upon me. But I remained steadfast, making petitions for these pagan people. I built on their local teachings, expanding their knowledge of God through images from nature; the three-leaved shamrock served as a symbol of the triune Godhead. By the end of my fast, I determined that upon those shores, walking those hills, I would live out my days in ministry for their souls.

From the early days of my kidnaping in chains, I returned now to bear insults, even hatred against my cause. To some I became a hero, yet others saw me as a soldier of God, fighting against unfriendly kings, working wonders against Druids, bringing the dead back to life, and calling upon the elements to serve me at will. With my staff raised high, I created miracles and wonders. Two such incidents occurred when I confronted King Loeguire.

The first instance was when I created a large bonfire in view of the Hill of Tara in celebration of my risen Lord. Little did I know that specific eve was meant for a pagan ritual where all fires were to be subdued in honor of the High King's flame. When the King demanded to know who lit the fire, one of his druids repeated a prophecy concerning the men that will come from over the sea with mantles over their heads and crooked-headed staves. All who hear them will answer them. The druid told the King that I, Patrick, was one of these men and must be rooted out immediately, saying, "If his fire is not put out, it will burn for a thousand years."

I was brought before King Loeguire where I explained that my presence in Ireland was to teach, yet the King rose in his arrogance, refusing me on all fronts. He prodded my faith, saying I should be tested by his two best druids, Lochru and Lucetmael, to decide my fate. I reflected on how some considered me a fierce evangelist. I had learned that God's blessings were strong, yet in the face of gross injustice, I had often employed vehement curses bringing down the wrath of God.

Well, a righteous anger then burned deep within me as they spouted off blasphemous words about my God. I stood tall, raising my staff, and cried aloud in a fierce voice, "O Lord, who can do all things and who sent me here, may this impious man who blasphemes your name be carried up and out of here and die without delay." Lochru's eyes flew open as he suddenly was lifted up as if by a mighty wind to a great height then dropped. The man fell, head first on a stone, crashing his skull. Onlookers gathered there were much afraid. It was after this act that the King decided perhaps we should talk.

And so we did. Yet as we conversed about our diverse situations, the second druid, Lucetmael, spat into my wine. I spied this abusive deed and decided to pray over my drink, turning it to ice. When I upturned the cup, only the spit fell out. I blessed the drink again, returning it to wine. Lucetmael accosted me saying, "Let's work wonders on the plain." I accepted the challenge, knowing the feats of my God would put any works done by that man to shame.

The testing began, in the presence of all around the King that day. First the druid created a foot of snow which I quickly melted. Lucetmael raised his arms high, summoning darkness which I, in turn, dispelled, showing God as the True Light. After several more tests, the King finally declared we should undertake the Ordeal of Fire. Two huts were built: one of dry wood, the other of greenwood. I was placed into dry wood hut, with their intention that I would burn alive while Lucetmael was placed into greenwood hut. At the King's command, both huts were set on fire. I prayed aloud for a miracle, reciting scriptures for all to hear. I asked for power over the elements, to keep my body safe. It took only a few minutes before I was retrieved from the burning flames. I walked out whole, bearing no burns nor scorch marks. Yet when I looked at Lucetmael's hut, there was nothing left but a pile of ashes.

I prayed for the lost souls of these men, yet knew God was teaching this King a powerful lesson. Loeguire then committed my new religion into law, saying, "Better to believe than to die." He offered me sanctuary, yet as I left with my followers, we were tracked, like prey to be eaten. Legend says I transformed myself and my men into a herd of deer, using an ancient rite of shape-shifting. I will neither confess nor deny those allegations, but I will say that we lived to see another day. In fact, I wrote a piece referred to as "St. Patrick's Breastplate" or "Lorica" as a hymn of protection:

> I bind myself today
>
> The strong name of the Trinity.

By invocation of the same,

The Three in One, and One in Three.

I bind this day to me forever.

I arise today

Through the strength of heaven;

Light of sun,

Radiance of moon,

Splendor of fire,

Speed of lightning,

Swiftness of wind,

Depth of sea,

Stability of earth,

Firmness of rock.

I arise today.

CLOSING

My years in Ireland proved fruitful. By the end of my time upon this earth, God granted me the privilege of ordaining over three hundred bishops, three thousand ministers, and twelve thousand lay men. I spent most of days in Armagh where I took on the Irish as my own sons and daughters. May I be remembered as a passionate yet simple man, generous of spirit, but fierce concerning issues of justice and slavery. I believe God allowed my early experiences to render my heart full of compassion for those in need. I leave you now with this tender blessing:

The love and affection of the angels be to you,

The love and affection of the saints be to you,

The love and affection of heaven be to you,

To guard you and to cherish you.

May God shield you on every steep,

May Christ aid you on every path,

May Spirit fill you on every slope,

On hill and on plain. Amen.

Julian

of

Norwich

Sacred Celtic Cross

OPENER: Good morning. I bid you welcome in the name of Mary, Holy Mother of God, and in the name her risen Son. I, Dame Julian of Norwich, offer you my story, a life granted by His grace, and no more, for Christ is the Cause of Enlightenment.

PART ONE: Personal Background / Petitions

My life before my years of ministry is of little consequence; why even my given name has disappeared from the church rosters, replaced with "Julian," the name of the saint whose church into which I freely gave myself for service in the small town of Norwich, England. My childhood was filled with pleasurable lessons in reading and writing where I nurtured my imagination. In my early twenties, my insatiable questioning concerning matters of the soul led me into prayer, deep meditations upon the scriptures, and many solitary wanderings. I pondered the existence of sin, the need for Christ's cruel crucifixion, and the possible glories awaiting believers in the life following our time in this physical body.

This process of queries led me to make three petitions of my God, only to be granted should they be in accordance with His benevolent will for me.

First, I wanted to have bodily sight of the physical pains of my Saviour upon the cross, to know the compassion of Mary as she stood by him, to experience what his disciples saw of His pain, and to suffer with Him, for I would be one of them. Through this petition I would have more the true mind of the Passion of Christ.

Second, I freely desired upon myself an illness, at the age of thirty, so close to death that I would be given the rites of the Church. I would believe that I was dying, as would all who saw me. Yet this illness would not carry me past this world, rather to the fullest extent barring the leaving of the soul. In this I would know the suffering and travails of the cross where there is no comfort, but all manner of bodily pains. This would be evident so that I might be purged, by the mercy of God. Afterwards I could live more to worship God because of that illness; for I wished to be more mindful of God.

Lastly, I asked for three gifts available only from God: contrition, kind compassion, and a steadfast longing towards God.

Now, you may ask yourself why a young woman might wish such things to come to her? I tell you in truth, my desire to know the fulness of God was so pervasive, that all else in life paled. So to my yearning heart, God granted my requests.

PART TWO: ILLNESS / NEAR-DEATH EXPERIENCE

At the age of thirty, yes, the same age as when our Lord Jesus began His evangelical ministry on this earth, I became afflicted with a weakening of the body so intense that all around me believed I was dying. I felt it a great sorrow to die so young. Yet I trusted in God's mercy and believed this illness was in accordance with His will. As my body became numb from the waist down, I asked to be set up on pillows to free up my heart in my last hours. I had told no one of my prayerful petitions. After three days and three nights, the Curate was called. I closed my eyes; I could not speak. Yet my soul rang out within me.

Be the angels of heaven shielding me,

The angels of heaven this night,

Be the angels of heaven keeping me

Soul and Body alike.

Be Thou a smooth way before me,

Be Thou a guiding star above me,

Be Thou a keen eye behind me,

This day, this night, forever.

On the fourth evening, the Curate administered the Holy Rites. He brought the cross and held it before my face saying, "I have brought thee the Image of thy Master and Saviour; look upon it and comfort thyself." I opened my eyes and gazed upon the crucifix. The room suddenly darkened, as if night had fallen, save for the light that emanated from the Curate's cross. My eyesight began to fail, leading me into utter darkness, while my upper body began to die. The heart slowed its beating while the breath came in shallow rhythms. I had scarcely any feeling throughout my entire body.

And then I died.

Suddenly all pain was gone, and I felt whole like never before. The pains of my body ceased, and I marveled at the change, thinking God had delivered me from this world. All sorrows melted away, leaving me with a sense of a lightness of being, a bliss beyond imagining. I was in the past, the present, and the future, for all time was One. Then I breathed once more to life on this earthly plane. Fifteen visions, or showings as I came to call them, were granted to me that day. I shall now share a few of these with you.

PART THREE: SHOWINGS

Christ on the Cross

One of my petitions was to know the pain of my Lord's Passion, his time on the cross, and to experience the suffering of his loved ones, Mary and his disciples. Several visions occurred with such profound clarity, placing me at the foot of the cross. The weather was wondrous cold with a hard, dry wind. As I looked upon the bleeding head of Jesus, the garland of thorns which had been placed on His head caused red blood to trickle down: hot, fresh, so much blood. I found myself in awe that one so revered within the Trinity would be made flesh. Drops of blood like thick, brown-red pellets thinned to bright red as they trickled down His brow.

My Saviour's face began changing color though it was covered with dried blood. This desecrated face reminded me of the foul black deeds of man upon Jesus's fair being, brown and black now rather than the fairest of heaven, the fruit of the Maiden's womb. His countenance changed with travail and sorrows.

> O sacred head now wounded, with grief and shame weighed down
>
> Now scornfully surrounded, with thorns thine only crown.
>
> How pale art thou with anguish, with sore abuse and scorn!
>
> How does thy visage languish, which once was bright as morn.

I must tell you that I was horrified by the scene. To see this tender body, broken. The plenteous blood flowed so there was no longer skin nor wound, just blood, for his blood flowed over all the earth for the salvation of mankind, flowing even into Hell and freeing the bonds of those captives. The Pain upon the cross was bitter, sharp, and long-lasting. It filled me with great sorrow to see such violence.

While His spirit remained, there was pain.

How could my own pain be any greater than to see the One who means everything to me suffer? He who remains all my life, all my bliss, all my joy? I knew then how little my pain was in comparison now to those of Christ. I repented for my petition - for had I known the truth of what I requested I would not have asked. I saw the compassion of Mary as she stood nearby, for she and Christ were so united that the greatness of her loving equaled the greatness of her pain. I wondered about the disciples' pain, for even the least of them loved Christ more than I could say.

Yes, Jesus made himself low for our sake. But through this death, I saw the height and nobility of the glorious Godhead, for as He was most tender and pure, so was He strong and mighty to suffer. This filled me with joy to honor His sacrifice: to see the mightiest, highest, noblest become meek and low . . . for us.

God Keeps Us In All Manner

Another set of visions confirmed how God will keep us in all manner of things. Whether in times of well-being, such as endless joy, or in times of woe, when temptations of the flesh become heavy and irksome.

For one who knew the bliss that is to come, I discovered a duality of this inward/outward struggle during my recovery. Soulful rest, after experiencing the bliss of heaven, leaves all else pale in comparison. At times, I felt a heaviness and weariness of this life. No comfort could ease my pain but faith, hope, and love; yet even these were not strong within me.

One afternoon Christ gave me comfort so blissful that I sensed no bodily pains. But suddenly the bodily pains returned, and I found myself vacillating between the two states of being twenty times. I cried out to be delivered. Yet this visceral teaching showed me that regardless of whether the soul is in comfort or in woe, God keeps us in both states.

In another vision concerning the nature of sin, it became known to me that if sin had not been, we should all have been clean and like to our Lord since he made us. But He pointed out the need for sin, stating, "All shall be well, and all shall be well, and all manner of things shall be well."

To clarify this point, an image of a hazelnut was given to me concerning God as The Keeper of All Things. The hazelnut stood for all that is made. As I wondered how it could last, the reply came: "It lasts because God loves it." For there were three properties: God made it, God loves it, and God will keep it. So God is Maker, Lover, Keeper. This hazel nut image calls us to be mindful that all things are important due to God's love.

Other Insights

Several visions dealt with the Trinity: The high Might of the Trinity is the Father, the deep wisdom of the Trinity is the Mother, and the love of the Trinity is our Lord. As for mothers, why God is both Father and Mother to us all. For as a mother nurtures her baby at her breast, so we lean against the Saviour and are fed with the spiritual food of the sacrifice of His body and blood. This shows us the nature of Motherhood through the Maiden's womb, meek and mild, in loving relation to her children.

As for true, soulful rest, often we seek rest in little things rather than God, who is The Very Rest Himself. This causes unrest in our heart and soul. We appease this imbalance through prayer where we unite the soul to God. Additionally, in prayer is the attitude of thankfulness: a true inward knowing with great reverence. Even in low times, by rehearsing His blessed passion and great goodness, the virtue of God's word turns into the soul and quickens the heart. For Truth sees God, Wisdom beholds God, and Love delights in God. So until we empty ourselves of all things, for love's sake, only then can we find spiritual rest. It was told to me that this is the natural yearning of our soul: to reconnect with our Maker. My soul sang out to my God:

Be thou my vision O lord of my heart

Naught be all else to me save that Thou art -

Thou my best thought by day or by night,

Waking or sleeping thy presence my light.

God Overcomes and Protects Us From the Enemy

I had fifteen visions total that day, but there was one to come, for I faced a fiend in my dreams on the following night. During the showings, all pain had ceased, yet the pain returned at end of the fifteenth showing. I was still somewhat blind and feeble, my head filled with a din of noise as the rest of my body ached as before. I moaned, as a wretched creature, dry and barren of comfort. A religious person came to visit, and when asking how I fared, I replied that I had raved today. He laughed heartily. Then I said I thought the Curate's cross had bled fast before me. The man sobered immediately. I realized my recklessness and was sore ashamed. When I saw he took it earnestly and with great reverence, I wept full, thinking, "Why would a priest believe me, for I don't believe it myself?"

But that night, as I slept, I dreamed. A fiend with the face of a young man sat upon my chest. His face was long and lean but red, like new-burnt tiles. His hair was rust red, clipped in front with full locks hanging about his temples. He grinned maliciously, showing white teeth. He had no hands but rather paws and gripped my throat with them as if to strangle me, yet he did not.

For even in my sleep I trusted to be saved, kept by the mercy of God. And by God's grace, He caused me to waken. Those around me saw my temples wet with sweat, yet my heart felt at ease. Suddenly I saw a smoke coming in the door followed by a great heat and foul stench. I cried out, "Benedicite Domine! It is all on fire here!" But when I asked those with me if they saw this fire, they said no. Relieved, I said, "Blessed be God. For while I slept, a fiend came to tempt me, but now all has vanished." This happened once more, yet once again I was quickly delivered.

Then Jesus showed me my soul: an endless world, a blissful kingdom. I saw a worshipful City with the majesty of the Trinity sitting in the center. The Godhead rules and sustains heaven with the pleasure of the Trinity in the making of Man's soul. So it is that our soul will never be satisfied by things that are beneath itself, things less than this spiritual union. For in man's soul is God the Maker's dwelling place, and the light and City are the Love of our Lord. He wills that our hearts be raised above the deepness of the earth and all vain sorrows to rejoice in Him.

I was brought to great rest and peace, without sickness of body.

This closed all the other visions. Jesus told me that he had sent the other fifteen visions to encourage me, to know them well; for they were not ravings, but truth. I was to take it, believe it, and comfort myself with it. Trust, and I shall not be overcome.

He wills that our souls be in Blissful Cheer.

PART FOUR: LIFE FOLLOWING THE VISIONS

You can see now why I spent the rest of my life in service to my Lord. I remained as anchoress at the Church of St. Julian where I wrote down these visions and insights relayed to me. I counseled those who sought me. My family could rest in the assuredness that I was safe, nestled in my cell and the loving arms of my Jesus. For they saw my face at every mass through the altar window and were able to visit with me.

After I recovered, I considered how God had answered all three petitions with this illness which traversed me from this world into the life awaiting all true believers. As petitioned, I had become gravely ill, nearly dying, at age thirty. Through physical pain I became acquainted with Christ's Passion. Then I received the gifts of contrition, compassion and longing for God through the visions that followed. I learned to be sympathetic with Him, and compassionate of His earthly sufferings, being more loving to all I met.

CLOSING:

God's blessing be yours,

And well may it befall you;

Christ's blessing be yours,

And well be you entreated;

Spirit's blessing be yours,

And well spend you your lives,

Each day that you rise up,

Each night that you lie down.

The guard of the God of life be thine,

The guard of the loving Christ be thine,

The guard of the Holy Spirit by thine,

To cherish thee,

To aid thee,

To enfold thee.

Amen.

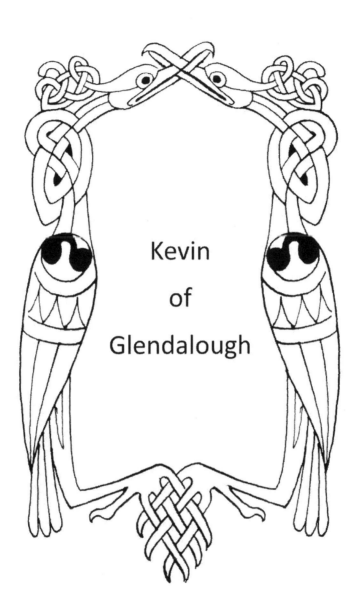

Kevin

of

Glendalough

GLENDALOUGH

Waterfalls,
glens, lakes,
mountain
valleys

SAINT KEVIN MONOLOGUE

HYMN : Fairest Lord Jesus, Ruler of all nature

O Thou of God and Man the Son,

Thee will I cherish, Thee will I honor,

Thou my soul's glory joy and crown.

OPENER : Many who know of my life in my beloved
Wicklow Mountains at Glendalough would be surprised to know
that I, Kevin, the modest monk presiding over Evensong, was
actually born into the lineage of the Irish Kings of Leinster. My
simple life in that lush valley was filled with prayerful meditations,
study of the scriptures, and wanderings in my solitary home
abundant with majestic waterfalls, wildflower meadows, and two
rippling lakes where the Red Deer drink their fill amidst the
splashing sounds of friendly otters. It is from God's handiwork and
time spent in solitudes there that I heard my Master's voice,

learned the quiet lessons from the natural world, and shared these heart insights with visiting pilgrims and diligent scholars.

EARLY LIFE

My beginnings were quite prestigious since my parents, Caemlug and Caemell, were both of the royal line. From my early childhood, I remember that my mother often regaled me with stories of when she carried me in her womb, claiming that her robust health and lack of pain was a miracle.   But a clear sign of mystery occurred on the day I was born. Heavy snows blanketed the village, yet those giant flakes melted in mid-air around our home. I had three siblings, for I was her fourth son, and she could not have been more proud.

When I was baptized, the name chosen by my parents was not the name given to me. The officiating priest, St. Cronan, later told me his version of what happened at the baptismal font.

"Remember it so well, I does, since I've never seen the likes of it again. Why there were angels, I tell you, a dozen of 'em glowing brighter than all the sanctuary candles. One angel tells me to be sure to name the boy Kevin which means 'beautiful, shining birth.' So, I whispered this to your parents, wondering what I should do since Kevin was not the name your parents had chosen. They told me I was crazy! Said they only heard a blackbird's song ringing from the rafters but saw nor heard anything more. Well, I rubbed my eyes, hoping the vision would go away, but that did me no good. Them angels were still there - quite persistent they was - about the name. So before anyone could stop me, I did as they bid me. And lad, you've been Kevin ever since." He would tousle my hair, give me a wink then carry on with his duties.

My mother rarely spoke of those infant days, yet once she did tell me a curious tale about a cow that wondrously appeared whenever I was hungry. As a wee babe, my belly could not tolerate my mother's milk. I was fed by a white cow, yet none knew the origin of this cow. Some villagers speculated it was a magical cow since it also sported red ears like those in the old faerie tales. But my mother, not believing in such things, would say that St. Brighid herself provided nourishment for this remarkable son.

In my childhood years, there were times when my mother would look at me with a distant gaze in her eyes, as if passing through the veil of years back to the time of my birth. "He said you would be special," she told me, "Patrick, the man of God, told me and your father that you would perform miracles like healing the sick, even raising some from the dead. He knew you would be smart, a man of letters, and one day be able to teach others in a place of great learning for strangers and pilgrims alike." Then she would wrap her arms around me, as if to stop time itself because she knew if the prophecy were to come true, I would be leaving her.

Despite her motherly affections, at the age of seven, I was sent to a monastery in Cornwall directed by St. Petroc to begin my education. Under the tutelage of three monks, Brothers Eoghan (Erin), Lochan, and Eanna, I learned my letters, memorized scriptures, and grew steadily in the ways of the Lord. I remember often hearing the song of a blackbird outside my quiet cell window, adding notes of natural inspiration to my studies. I rose each morning to the calls of nature, and prayed most fervently to my God:

Bless to me, O God

My heart and my speech,

And bless to me, O God,

The handling of my hand;

Strength and busyness of morning,

Habit and temper of modesty,

Force and wisdom of thought,

And Thine own path, O God of virtues,

Till I go to sleep this night.

After a full day, following the service for Evensong, I would close the day with this prayer:

Thou King of moon and sun,

Thou King of stars beloved,

Thou Thyself knowest our need

O Thou merciful God of life.

I was a quiet, serious lad yet I respected my elders and was loved in return. When I became of age, I took my vows as a monk and entered the dedicated service to my Lord.

FIRST YEARS AT GLENDALOUGH

The time came for me to leave my brethren in search of my own path in this world. In my studies, I had learned of the "green martyrdom" which followed the strict, ascetic practices of the penitent pilgrim. To fully devote myself to God, I opted to follow this discipline wherever I landed.

As a lad, I had discovered that I could hear the gentle voices of the 'Shining Ones' or angels, those ministers of God whose whispers of wisdom served me daily. They offered me comfort, friendship, and solace. When it came time for me to leave, I asked for their Divine Aid to show me the way in which I should go. Direction came, so I sailed back to Ireland, back to Leinster where I sought not village life but the sanctity of the wilderness. I was led to Glendalough, its own name meaning "Valley of the Two Lakes." The Lower Lake held lush vegetation rimming the waters, yet it was shelter I needed, so I continued on the path towards the Upper Lake where I discovered a small cave. This rock fortress became my home.

I learned to love my life of solitude and remained at Glendalough with only the angels and animals for my companions for seven years. Since I had always been closer to animals than people, this served my purposes quite well. I had studied much about the natural world from the monks and was no stranger to living off the land with a simple diet based on the turnings of seasons. Like the red squirrels chittering nearby, I gathered nuts in autumn from oak and hazel trees then feasted on delicious black berries from the Bilberry shrubs in summer. I also created savory soups with herbs such as wood sorrel, primrose, and wild garlic. Both lakes were abundant in fish, supplying food not only for me but also the Greylag Geese. These feathered friends returned every winter, whose honks and antics were quite entertaining!

I marveled at God's bounty, ready for the taking. I recited blessings such as this ancient rite over salads of Club Moss and Silverweed which sustained me:

Honey under ground

Silverweed of spring.

Honey and condiment

Whisked whey of summer.

Honey and fruitage

Carrot of autumn.

Honey and crunching

Nuts of winter

Between Feast of Andrew

And Christmastide.

Heavily forested woods of oaks, hawthorns, and rowans became my sanctuary. Tall yew and aspen trees offered shelter from winter rains, blending with the constant curtain of evergreen holly. During spring and summer, the leaf-filled branches rose towards heaven filled with songs of the plentiful Wood Warblers and Blue Tits. I marveled at the shy Red Deer who often followed me as silent partners in the green world.

I particularly enjoyed the summer colorful carpet joining the two lakes: a profusion of wild flowers such as purple Dog-Foot Violets, Bluebells, Yellow Flag Irises, and the pure whites of Wild Angelica. Pink and purple heather covered the nearby mountain slopes. It was feast for my eyes!

I often meditated in the silvery birch groves surrounding the Upper Lake, wading chest-high into its cold waters, following the practice of many saints before me, becoming one with nature. I would sing hymns for my Lord:

HYMN: Fair are the meadows, fairer still the woodlands,

Robed in the blooming garb of spring;

Jesus is fairer, Jesus is purer

Who makes the woeful heart to sing.

ENCOUNTER WITH WILD ANIMALS

My time at Glendalough also revealed my steady connection to animals through the preserving grace of God my Father. I mentioned my steady diet of fish; however, the best part of fishing was yet to come.

I often stood at the water's edge in prayer, meditating on the psalms I read in my breviary or "psalter." Well, one day I ventured so far into the silences that I accidentally dropped my book into the water then much to my dismay, watched it sink into the depths of the Upper Lake. Books were precious, and I deeply mourned its loss. I cried aloud, bemoaning my grief, when suddenly I heard a ruckus of splashing water. I looked out to see what appeared to be a small animal heading my way, swimming vigorously through the waves. Imagine my surprise when a bright-eyed otter trotted out of the water and dropped the book at my feet. He remained still, gazing up at me with what I can only describe as a smile upon his face. I bowed in thankfulness then watched as he turned quickly about and disappeared into the water. I sat down on the sandy shore, amazed by this unexpected act of kindness. But more astonishing was that the book was completely dry!

That was the first of many encounters with this joyful creature who would often bring me fresh fish, dropping them at my feet as he had the book. Years later, once pilgrims and buildings arrived to create the monastery, a greedy young man attempted to kill this otter to make a pair of fine gloves. It was as if my friend discerned the danger, so he disappeared, never to be seen again. It left me feeling bereft of such a gentle and steady companion.

It always brought me joy in late summer to see the Red Deer mothering their new fawns, the eager little ones nursing then growing in grace into the gentle nature of their breed. Once I found myself in need of "mother's milk" and one of those wonderful creatures assisted me. A neighboring chieftain sent his son Faelain to be fostered by me since curses had been laid on his previous sons. I graciously accepted the child yet knew no wet nurses were to be found. I prayed, and in answer to that prayer, a milking doe came to me and loosed her milk into the hollow of a stone. She arrived every morning, every evening, until the child was ready for solid food. Thus the child was nourished in the glory of God.

PRIMARY ANIMAL: BLACKBIRD

Perhaps the most astonishing event with animals happened with my totem animal: the blackbird. This bird's song rang out during my baptism and later comforted me during my monastic studies. It came as no surprise that my solitary life lent itself towards the animal which ancient Celts believed symbolized the Gateway into Spiritual Realms or The Inner Call.

The most unusual encounter with this bird occurred in the spring. Near the shores of the Upper Lake, I built a small hut to be used in the spring and summer time to provide ample shelter from storms and heavy rains. I laid mica schist flagstones as a flooring then added rushes on top with a cotton blanket to create a simple pallet.

It was the beginning of Lent, a period most sanctified by the church. As I entered into prayer for this time of reflection upon the values of repentance, a miracle began. As I lay upon the flagstones with arms outstretched in a cruciform style, a small blackbird landed in my open palm. I acknowledged its presence but resumed my prayers. It then flew away, only to return time and time again with small grasses and leaves, twigs and stems, until a nest appeared in my hand. I remained very still, not wanting to disturb this determined mother. It was not long after that she lay four eggs in her well-constructed nest then proceeded to keep them warm until their hatching.

Being Lent, I chose to remain prone, in my hut, and show the same dedication to deliverance as my blackbird friend. I was fed droplets of water along with berries and nuts by my animal community. Ignoring angelic protests that I should rise, I pondered the pain of my Lord upon the cross. After fourteen days, the babies hatched successfully where they were then spirited away by angelic hands to the safety of a nearby tree.

LESSONS FROM THE ANIMALS

Over the years, I learned to honor all of creation as God's handiwork by seeing His goodness in them. I acknowledged the evidence of God's Divine Presence when I spent time with these beings, perceiving each one with dignity and grace as partners in God's world. A deep affection for these creatures grew within me, for He who created them created me as well. I passed these lessons along to all who would listen, disciples and lay folk alike.

Animals provide inspiration along with their knowledge of the past. We learn from animals at a soul level that connects us all. The beasts who attended me knew God's goodness within my soul; they trusted me. They allowed me to transform into an example of living with intention, living as one with our environment. I remembered the ancient words of connection with the natural world: "The strength, tenacity, grace, and beauty of all creatures are ours to access if we meet them on equal terms."

HYMN: This is my Father's world, and to my listening ears

All nature sings and round me rings

the music of the spheres.

This is my Father's world: I rest me in the thought

Of rock and trees, of skies and seas;

His hand the wonders wrought.

This is my Father's world, the birds their carols raise

The morning light, the lily white,

   declare their Maker's praise.

This is my Father's world: He shines in all that's fair;

In the rustling grass I hear Him pass,

He speaks to me everywhere.

RETURN TO SOCIETY

You may think it strange for one so studious to remain in seclusion for so long, not sharing the knowledge he gleaned from spiritual teachings. I was content in my solitude, yet a local farmer named Dimma changed my heart, changed my life.

Dimma's cow often came to my cave, showing his devotion to me by licking my feet and clothes while I sat in prayer. Dimma noticed that his cow gave more plentiful milk following his "disappearances," so he charged his herdsman to follow the cow to uncover the mystery. By that time, due to my lack of proper nourishment, I was weak beyond measure and had sought shelter in a nearby tree hollow, willing God to either take me or supply assistance. My prayer was answered.

The herdsman discovered me in my oaken tomb, and after seeing my ill state, departed saying he would return with help. Dimma and his man took me out on a litter, yet the going was strenuous through the heavily forested area. When they asked me for help, I prayed aloud that God would grant us smooth and clear passage. The two men were completely amazed as "invisible hands" widened the path by pulling back limbs and branches until I had passed then settled back to their normal state.

Once in the farmer's home, they nursed me back to health. The family, pagan by tradition, began asking questions about my life at Glendalough. They were eager to hear more of God's wonders, yearning for His teachings. Just like the angelic aid broadened the forest trail, a new path back to society was now being cleared.

My teachings were shared with neighbors who told their friends and before long, I had a following. Seeing the need for a place for teaching, I sought assistance. Since King O'Toole of Glendalough was pagan, he would not concede the property for a monastery. However, he struck a deal with me. His favored goose, due to its old age, was not long for this world. The King asked me to restore this goose to its youthfulness, and if I could do that, then he would grant me whatever land over which the goose flew. I prayed - the goose grew young - he flew over the entire valley of Glendalough, thus sealing the deal.

After seeking monastic assistance, I became an ordained an abbott with a following of disciples. Local farmers began constructing stone foundations for the monastery. We located the primary settlement near my cave by the Upper Lake, naming it Teampull na Skellig or "Church of the Rock" which was accessible only by boat. In later years, an entire collection of stone buildings was erected by the Lower Lake: a cathedral for worship, smaller churches for study, a cemetery, and a round tower. Fellow monks joined me in my pursuits now, and I welcomed the company of men once more.

WONDERS AND MIRACLES

Throughout my life, I saw God's wonders and miracles worked out before me. The element of abundance happened to me during my monastic studies. I gave away food intended for crop gatherers to an unexpected group of pilgrims. When rebuked for this act by my superiors, I asked that all ale jars be filled with water and bare bones be gathered. I lifted my hand to the Lord over this spread: the water turned to ale and the bones regained their meat.

Sometimes miraculous healings would occur. A young village lad was struck down with epilepsy, and it was revealed that his cure would come from apples grown at Glendalough. However, we had no apple trees. So once again I prayed to God for his sustenance and healing Hand. My prayer was answered as our willow trees began to produce apples! The young boy was cured, and the willows continued to bear fruit for many years to come.

In all the years of service, my dearest friend was Saint Ciaran who built his own monastic site in the center of Ireland named Clonmacnoise. The ancient Celts would call us anam cara or "soul friends." When I heard of my friend's imminent death, I immediately made haste to his side. How distressed I became when I heard he died two days prior to my arrival. According to his wishes, his monks had laid him out in his church until my arrival. As I stood there, mourning over the loss of so dear a friend, his body trembled and then glowed with a great light. He opened his eyes once again as his spirit returned, breathing normally as if nothing had happened! We visited together for quite some time then Ciaran instructed me to administer the Eucharist to him. I did, with tears in my eyes, as my friend said his last blessing, offering me his silver bell as a sign of our lasting unity. Then he took leave of this earth for good, and I returned home, marveling once again at the true wonders of our God.

Years flew by; my hair silvered while I continued to teach all who came, all who would listen. I never tired of walking in the woods I had come to love so deeply, listening for the call of the blackbird or the rustling of leaves when the Red Deer passed. Never could I imagine, having been so close to dying when Dimma found me in that oak tree, that I would live a long and healthy life spanning almost one hundred and fourteen years.

HYMN: Fair is the sunshine, fairer still the moonlight,

And all the twinkling starry host;

Jesus shines brighter, Jesus shines purer,

Than all the angels heaven can boast.

Amen.

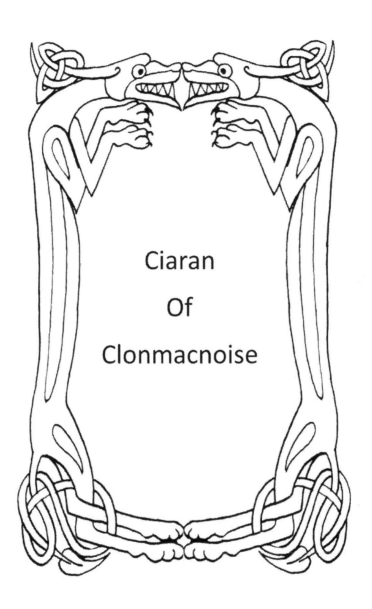

Ciaran

Of

Clonmacnoise

Clonmacnoise
Monastery

Round Tower
(River Shannon)

St. Ciaran's Chapel

PART ONE: EARLY FAMILY LIFE AND MONASTIC TRAINING

OPENING: 9th cent. Traditional Irish blessing

A Scribe in the Woods

A hedge of trees surrounds me,

A blackbird's song enchants me;

Above my lined page

Birds make a song for me.

The gray-mantled cuckoo

Sings in the bushes;

May God protect me -

I write well in the greenwood.

I welcome you this day in the name of my Lord, the savior of my soul. I am Ciaran, son of Beiot and Darerca from Roscommon, Ireland. Many of you may know me through my association with the monastery at Clonmacnoise, that seat of monastic learning in the center of Erin whose ripples reach across the country through the lives of disciples and students. Let me tell you now how I came to be there, to teach there, and to live there.

FAMILY BACKGROUND

My family always encouraged learning: through books, through experiences. I used to love hearing Grandfather recite his poetry or rant about some bloke who lived quite a long time ago, riling up folks. But mostly I loved the Bible stories, tales about heroic deeds done by good people. I would ponder those tales while I tended the sheep and cows, a practice which left much time for considering one's place in the world. Although I also I helped my father, a carpenter by trade, as he bent the hard grain of wood to his will into chariot wheels or tools for neighbors, somehow I knew the farming life was not for me. Instead, I preferred to sit at the feet of our local priest, Justus, the man who baptized me, peppering him with questions about the spiritual life. He found me to be an apt student. He taught me the power of prayer and how to be humble before my God.

I enjoyed rambling through the dense woodlands with folks who would teach me the names of each plant, each flower, each tree. My love of learning served me well even in such an informal setting as I recited the names, committing them to memory. I felt a deep connection with this aspect of my Blessed King, God the Creator, and this relationship served me throughout my life. It reminds me of a wonderful Irish blessing:

May the King shield you in the valleys

May Christ aid you on the mountains,

May Spirit bathe you on the slopes,

In hollow, on hill, on plain

Mountain, valley and plain.

May the Father take you

In His fragrant clasp of love.

As a young lad, I began to see the miracles of God all around me. When I was twelve, I came upon Oengus, the King's son, kneeling in deep sorrow beside his favorite horse. The poor creature had just died, and when I saw the depth of connection between the two, I took a bold step to ease the lad's pain. I found some water, prayed over it then sprinkling this blessed water over the horse I asked that it be restored. To the surprise of Oengus and those gathered around, the horse immediately began to breathe once more; he rose then stood beside his dearest master.

Another incident occurred when my mother scolded me for not remembering to bring her back some honey following my trip to the village bee hives. Suddenly an idea came to me. I took an earthen jar to the well, filled it with water and blessed it, asking that the water be turned to honey. Sure enough, don't you know it turned gold before my very eyes into the sweetest honey my mother had ever tasted.

My third experience with the power of prayer was born out of sacrifice and need. I was delivering a cauldron to our neighboring liege, King Furban, when I came upon a family deep in the woods with little to their name. Their hut resembled a bird's broken nest rather than a structure providing shelter while their meager stores where almost barren. I knew this family could have a hot meal if they only had the means to cook over an open hearth. I gifted the cauldron to them instead of following orders from my father. When the King heard of this, he was outraged. Top pay off the debt, he threw me into his cooking work force grinding flour in his mill. As I stood by the quern, considering the injustice of my situation, I prayed, and suddenly the great mill stone began to turn on its own accord. Image my astonishment! When the news spread, I was brought before King Furban who informed me that the debt was now paid, not only from the event at the mill but also because he was gifted that very morning with three cauldrons. I was never so happy to be sent home.

MONASTIC TRAINING AT CLONARD

After these miracles and my keen thirst for spiritual learning, my parents decided to send me for monastic training. At age thirteen I traveled to Clonard to study with Saint Finnian, bringing with me a favorite dun cow and her calf as payment for my tuition fee. The cow was blessed with an abundance of milk, so for many years, my classmates and I never thirsted. She was such a tender creature, and one who served our monastery both in life and in death. Following her natural passing, it was suggested that we use her tanned hide as a binding for a book of psalms while the rest was kept as a covering for warmth. I was more than pleased when I discovered that those resting within the comforting embrace of that fur were also healed of any infirmities!

I knew early on that my love for nature and all its creatures was a solid thread in my soul. I came to know the depth of those connections in some very interesting ways. While at Clonard, I often wrote upon a slate with messages for my tutor, Finnian. I befriended a red fox who would carry the satchel with my slate inside between Finnian and myself. All went well until the mischievous fellow became distracted by the satchel strap between his black lips. He stopped to chew on it only to discover a sudden pack of hounds well on his heels. He came flying back to me, finding safety in the folds of my monastic robes when I sent the dogs away. I stroked his red fur, alleviating the fears in his trembling body and opted to never put him in harm's way again.

I also came to know a stag quite well. This stag would stand beside me, in regal stillness, and allow me to place my book in his antlers as a reading lectern. This was highly unusual for such a noble beast to offer service. I found it quite comfortable to attend to my studies in this way. Although, there was the time that a sudden squall thundered in the distance, startling the stag. He ran into the woods, taking my precious psalter with him. You can imagine my dismay since books were at such a premium. I feared that even if I saw it again, the pages would be wet and ruined beyond repair. However, when the rains ceased the next day, who should appear but my four-footed friend, still carrying my book in his antlered rack. I stroked his neck in appreciation for returning my book and was greatly amazed to find the pages completely dry without any damage at all. How marvelous is our Great Creator!

HYMN: All Things Bright and Beautiful

[Refrain] All things bright and beautiful,

all creatures great and small,

all things wise and wonderful -

the Lord God made them all.

Each little flower that opens,

each little bird that sings -

God made their glowing colors,

God made their tiny wings.

God gave us eyes to see them,

and lips that we might tell

how great is God Almighty,

who has made all things well.

You recall my earlier occurrence with King Furban and the grinding mill? Well, something similar happened at Clonard. A great famine overtook the land, so all the students were charged with taking turns at the grinding wheel. We used only coarse oats, unable to afford the finer grained wheat. When my turn arrived, I carried the heavy bag of oats to the mill. Under that burden, I dreamed of wheat, the finest wheat, that could be made into the most delicious bread the lads had ever tasted. I spoke my dream aloud as I entered the mill, and who should hear me but the Shining Ones, known as angels to most. They told me to put the oats beneath the grinding stone, so I followed their instructions. As I turned the wheel, those oats transformed into wheat! When we made bread with this grain, we discovered it satisfied the deepest hunger and made the sick well again. Like the children of Israel who ate manna as they wandered in the desert, so we were fed for forty days and forty nights on this miraculous Bread of Heaven.

As the years passed, I enjoyed the fellowship with other students, especially a pleasing lad named Columcille with whom I shared a deep friendship. As I continued my studies with Finnian. I craved to know more of God's word, expanding His ways into the world, for the betterment of all. I spoke of this desire to Finnian who confessed that he had seen a vision of both Columcille and myself. The saint described two moons rising, one silver and one gold. Columcille was the golden sun whose love of learning would shine abroad while I was the silver moon due to my virtues and deeds. Finnian believed that both moons symbolized the rise of two great men in Ireland whose fame would spread throughout the world for many years to come. I was humbled by this news, but also inspired as I knew that my time at Clonard was now coming to a close.

PART TWO: TRAVELS AND SETTLEMENTS

SOLO TRAVELS

I packed my few belongings and with hope in my heart, walked west. As I traveled, I met many people. Whenever I saw a need, if I could help, I did. There was an ache in my spirit which spurred me further west. Many of my Irish contemporaries were establishing small monastic sites, places of learning and worship, yet I sensed no place of permanency for myself, not yet. I prayed fervently for God to open more doors of learning to me and soon heard of Saint Enda practicing on Inishmore, one of the three Aran Islands. My spirit quickened within me as I heard about his teachings and wonders, so I made haste across Erin to its western Atlantic shores.

I remember the smell of the cold, salt air as I boarded a small curragh taking me across the waters from the port in Doolin. The oarsman was a sturdy lad, denying any assistance on my part, so I sat back and enjoyed the ride. Fortunately, the seas were calm that day, rising in gentle currents which so often were much more formidable. As we approached the island and waters shallowed, I marveled at the crystalline waters, brilliant shades of turquoise rippling and melting into darker shades of cobalt blue. As we landed, I noticed the monastery built on the hillside and made my way up the winding path to the cloister: my next home.

Saint Enda was generous with me in his time and his teachings. We recognized within each other the desire to know God and all He had to offer. Our time together brought me closer to the fruition of Saint Finnian's vision of my sharing lessons and insights with others. I often walked the perimeter of the island, marveling at the stone enclosures for the vast number of sheep. I delighted in the solitudes of the sea which grew into my constant companion. When I became weary and thirsty, I would stop by a well whose waters had been blessed by Saint Enda and find myself invigorated once more. This well offered healing on many levels to all who drank from its depths.

As my restlessness resurfaced, Enda and I spoke about possibilities for my future where I could open a place of learning. One day, we shared a vision which we later called the Great Tree Vision. Never before had I experienced such a profound visual invitation from God. On a stream bank in the center of Ireland grew this tree - enormous in size and firm in structure. Its duty to protect all of Erin was symbolized through its expansive branches and extensive root system. Rich, sweet fruit hung in clusters ready for the taking by men and animals alike. We sat in silence, allowing every color, every detail to be etched on our minds and hearts.

It was Enda who interpreted this vision. He knew it symbolized the answer to my discontented spirit by offering me a permanent place. In that space, people would be nourished by the lessons I had learned, walk in the ways of the Lord, and share God's goodness with others by observing my own actions. He also said the place would stand for over one thousand years.

I was astounded as he spoke, yet his words struck a chord deep in my soul. My destiny now stood before me, no longer veiled in mists but seen with clarity. I knew God's timing would determine the exact spot, so I bid Enda farewell.

I ventured south and visited with a dear friend and spiritual mentor, Senan, on Scattery Island at his monastic site. The ascetic life there was more than familiar while the brethren were quite welcoming, and I enjoyed becoming a part of their community. I stayed for a short while, yet soon I felt the tug of travel, the vision of the tree beckoning me to continue my journey. I walked along the coastal roads leading towards the east. I met other pilgrims along the way, and some followed me to a small island, Inis

Ainghin or Hare Island, where I established my first monastery. We lived a simple life with a steady daily schedule of work, study, and practical chores. I delighted in the growth of our community and praised God again for His wonderful grace. I lived here for seven years, yet once again knew this was not the permanent place being held in readiness for me. I traveled north, into the very heart of Ireland.

PART THREE: THE VISION REVEALED

ESTABLISHING CLONMACNOISE MONASTERY

I came to a place named Cluain Mhic Nois, meaning "meadow of the Sons of Nois," whose fertile land along the banks of the River Shannon called to me. The green fields were perfect for grazing animals to support a large community while the town of Athlone was situated just south for ease of purchasing goods. As I enquired as to who owned this land, I was told that Prince Diarmit was the landholder, so I set up a meeting. I told the young prince of my plans to create a place of learning and sharing of God's holy wisdom. The Lord opened the man's heart who then gave the land over to me generously. I called him "King" as I sensed a shift in the prince's situation, and surely the next day did not his father die, raising Diarmit to the role of sovereign. I asked if he would share in driving the first wooden post of the primary foundational structure into the ground alongside me, believing that kings and men of learning could work together. Thus began a long and fruitful relationship.

The Dead at Clonmacnoise

In a quiet water'd land, a land of roses

Stand Saint Ciaran's city fair;

And the warriors of Erin in their famous generations

Slumber there.

There below the dewy hillside sleep the noblest

Of the clan of Conn,

Each below his stone with name in branching
    Ogham

And the sacred knot thereon.

There they laid to rest the seven Kings of Tara,

There the sons of Cairbre sleep

Battle-banners of the Gael that in Ciaran's plain of crosses

Now their final hosting keep.

(*14th cent. Poem by Angus O Giollain*)

DAILY LIFE

Ten disciples worked beside me to create a small cluster of structures made of either wood or stone which would serve us for shelter, worship, meals, and study. We started a garden with the help of neighboring farmers and were gifted animals for our needs. We built a pit where I asked that a constant flame be maintained, symbolic of the holy light burning within our community. I became the first abbot of Clonmacnaoise, instructing my followers in the ways of the simple lifestyle without distractions from our spiritual purposes. I replicated the daily routines of the previous monasteries I had visited whose ascetic lifestyle paired with my own beliefs. I confirmed my lessons through example. In time, my faith along with my attitudes towards prayer and fasting proved a valuable tool in mentoring those who studied with me. I taught them the values of labor, humility, and discipline, as well as our role as protector of the poor.

I was finally home.

ANAM CARA (SOUL FRIEND)

In this life we may be blessed with an "anam cara" or soul-friend. In my travels, I knew several such men who met me heart to heart, sharing our thoughts, our faith, our visions of a kinder world brought about by delivering God's messages of love. My early tutor Finnian was the first to teach me about this spiritual bond, through practice and experience. Both Columcille of Iona and Senan of Scattery Island knew the depths such a bond can carry for seeking council and support. Yet my truest friend was Kevin of Glendalough. I pray that when my time comes to leave this earthly plane that Kevin will be by my side. Perhaps I will gift him with my silver bell as symbol of the ties which bind us.

I have seen it - a miracle - where my body lies in wait for him to appear, then by angelic intervention, breath returns, bringing me back to life for a brief time to talk as we always did and share our deepest yearnings. I know many have succumbed to the yellow plague of late, and wonder if I, too, shall follow it to the grave. If so, I have instructed my disciples to lay me in the ground near the tree planted to symbolize my early vision of the Great Tree shared with Saint Enda. In this way, I return my body to nature from which it sprung while my soul shall rejoice with my Lord in heavenly realms.

CLOSING

HYMN: O for a thousand tongues to sing

My dear Redeemer's praise,

The glories of my God and King

The triumphs of His grace.

My gracious Master and my God,

Assist me to proclaim,

To spread through all the earth abroad,

The honors of Thy name.

Amen.

BIBLICAL BONUS:

MARY

MAGDALENE

OPENER: I stand before you today as Mary Magdalene, Apostle of the Apostles, and greet you all in the name of my risen Master, Jesus the Christ, Jesus the Messiah.

PART ONE

It seems that my identity prior to my Lord's death and resurrection has been clouded and obscured by theological conjectures drawn from the writings about the lives of the early Christians. But first, we must agree that any incident observed by more than one will reveal varying details, some even in contradiction with other accounts. Yet what we learn from the incident itself, rather than arguing over the minutia, is the more enlightened path.

We begin with a rather scandalous view of myself as a known sinner. Some equate that with a seducer of men, one who would anoint Jesus with perfumes which I used to arouse men's passions. Ah, the "woman with the alabaster jar" you say. Yes, well, even if I were that woman, the lesson to be learned here is one of great forgiveness. Jesus showed compassion and even offered the parable of the cancellation of debts for two people, saying the person with the greater debt would then show more compassion. Thus it is with redemptive love.

As for the anointing, there are three such accounts, and I cannot fully take credit for being in all three places. One says it was done by a prostitute in Simon's home, another by a sinful woman in the home of a Pharisee, and the last in Bethany at the home of Lazarus and his sisters Mary and Martha. Here Mary takes on the task of using nard and anointing the Master's feet, wiping them with her long hair. So, am I Mary of Bethany, the sister of Lazarus? John didn't think so since he differentiated between this Mary and the one from Magdala. Yet again, the anointing itself is the more critical point, as Jesus remarks that this act is in preparation of what lies ahead - his death and burial. The lesson here is one of service.

Yet the last assumption is that I was a wealthy woman from whom Jesus cast out seven demons. I believe in the future that maladies of the mind and emotions will no longer be viewed as demons, but still, definitely a condition in want of healing. Here it begins to make more sense that one who would survive such a life-changing transformation would follow the One responsible for restoration of wholeness in mind, body, and spirit. Here you would find a devoted woman, one willing to serve, an educated mind willing to learn from the greatest Master of all time.

And what of the rumors of wife to our Lord, the one whom He loved best, according to Peter? In the later writings of my friends Thomas and Philip, they recorded the humanity of Jesus, portraying me as his closest companion, using intimate language, even kissing me? But what can the letters of men reveal about the intimacies of a woman's heart? And if we were married, why should it mar Jesus's divinity? For he was both fully human and fully divine.

In all these roles prior to the Crucifixion, whether I be one Mary or represent them all as the Eternal Feminine in these stories, we must remember the truths displayed in each tale. For, we all are like gems with many facets, some sides shining more brightly than others. So who am I? I am a woman who loved a man, a follower who revered her Lord, and a messenger to the world that Jesus is risen.

But I am not the only one whose true identity brought questions. Even the Master often asked of His disciples, "Who do men say that I am?" They replied with various answers: a carpenter, a politician, a rebel, a poet, even the Son of God.

The Child of Glory, The Child of Mary,

Born in the stable, the King of all,

Who came to the wilderness

And in our stead suffered;

Happy they are counted who to Him are near.

We beheld Christ, the Spirit of truth,

The same drew us in 'neath the shield of His crown.

PART TWO

At the Cross

How it crushed my heart to see my dearest love hanging, like some criminal, upon that horrible wooden destroyer of life. Iron nails gouged through the center of His gentle hands and well-traveled feet. The mockery of the crowd appalled me, giving Him vinegar to drink then placing the thorny circlet upon His head, piercing His forehead and skull till rivers of blood ran like tears down His cheeks. They even jabbed a spear into His side. After hanging there for six hours, the sky darkened and remained as black as charred embers until three hours later when my Beloved cried out for His own Father. As His spirit left his body, lightning rent the sky as the earth quaked and shuddered at the atrocity of that death.

Once Jesus was taken off that dreadful cross, Joseph cleaned the body and wrapped it in linen. Joseph had a great stone rolled into place to cover the tomb's entrance, sobbing for the loss of his greatest friend. Yet Jesus' mother and I remained, in constant vigil outside the tomb. There was talk about Pilate's men guarding the tomb to ensure that none of us stole the body in order to claim a false resurrection. Guards were posted. But I stayed. Where else would I be?

I did leave at the end of the day to prepare the burial spices and ointments, and waiting after the Sabbath, returned early on the third morning with Jesus's mother and Johanna. As we returned to the tomb, the earth quaked once more. The guards fell down as if dead men while we held each other in fright until we saw two shining beings, angels. They stood beside the large rock enclosing the tomb and rolled it away. They stood there in such brilliant raiment that we fell to our feet before them. They asked, "Why do you seek the living among the dead? He is not here. Come inside, look for yourselves." We slowly walked through the dark stone opening and there saw only the grave clothes tumbled about on the floor. The angels spoke again saying, "Do you not recall Jesus's words saying He must be crucified, according to the prophecies, but on the third day, He would rise again? Run now, tell His disciples that He is risen and gone before you into Galilee where you shall see Him."

Heeding the angelic command, I ran with my heart racing faster than any wind knowing my Beloved was alive. No sooner did this thought cross my heart when I saw Him on the road. All strength left me as relief flooded my body. I could no longer stand, but rather sank to my knees. Mary, Johanna and I embraced His feet, crying tears of joy. He placed his hands upon my head in that reassuring way, and smiled at me, repeating the words of the angels: "Now go, tell the others to meet Me in Galilee." And then He was gone.

Because we were the first to receive this news, and I spoke so boldly for Him, some called me the "Apostle to the Apostles" for when I told them the news that Jesus had risen, they did not believe me. Even Peter ran to the grave, only to find an empty tomb. Earlier he even denied knowing Jesus three times, just as our Lord had said. They were afraid for their lives, knowing their Master had been cruelly murdered, so what lay in store for them? I could understand that fear but not their disbelief. I said, "Do not weep and grieve or let your hearts remain in doubt, for his grace will be with you all, sustaining and protecting you." Yet their courage returned after we met with Him, supped with Him, and discovered that He would leave us the Comforter, the Holy Spirit, to remain with us on earth. Then He took us all to Bethany one last time, and after blessing each one of us, He lifted his hands towards the heavens and disappeared. That was the last time I saw Him face to face. Once more, I could do nothing more than cry.

PART THREE

Once Jesus departed this earth for good, we all scattered, like seeds on the wind. I went with Mary, His mother, to Ephesus. Yet again there seems some dispute as to exactly where I spent the rest of my days. Some say I traveled as far as Marseilles, France, and remained for thirty years in a small house on a hill called La Sainte-Baume. But rather than live a totally secluded life, I shared my Beloved's teachings with all who would listen. I even wrote down the events that followed the resurrection, yet I fear my words will lie buried beneath the sands of time, light of these truths not visible for many generations to come.

I spent many hours in solitude and prayer, and it was during those times that my Lord would visit me in visions. My heart soared to the heights of holiness through this remarkable communion. Once I told Him, "Lord, I see You as a vision." He replied, "You are blessed since the sight of Me does not disturb you. For where the heart is, there is the treasure." He continued to tell me that we strive to be in alignment with our true nature, that is the image of God within us, namely the One Heart, the One Being, the One God who is All in All. Other lessons he taught me concerned the route of the soul, passing through levels of understanding to its final rest.

"From this moment on, I go forward into the season of the Great Age, the Aeon, and there, where Time rests in stillness in the Eternity of Time, I will repose in silence." [**From Gospel of Mary Magdalene]**

(Hymn: "Immortal Love")

Immortal Love, forever full, forever flowing free,

Forever shared, forever whole, a never-ebbing sea.

CLOSING

May I each day give love to Thee, Jesu,

Each night may I do the same;

Each day and night, dark and light

May I laud Thy goodness to me, O God.

Amen

APPENDIX: RESOURCES

RESEARCH AIDS

Carmichael, Alexander. Carmina Gaedelica: Hymns &
     Incoantations. Hudson, NY: Lindisfarne Press, 1992, [1900].

Carr-Gomm, Philip and Stephanie. The Druid Animal Oracle. NY:
     Fireside Pub., 1994.

Clonmacnoise. [Booklet]. Ireland: Government Publications of
     Ireland, 1994

Corkery, John. Cluain Chiarain: The City of Ciaran. Ireland: Turner's
     Printing, 1979.

Earle, Mary C. And Sylvia Maddox. Holy Companions: Spiritual
     Practices from the Celtic Saints. Harrisburg, NY:
     Morehouse Pub., 2004.

- - -. Praying with the Celtic Saints: Companions for the Journey.
     MN: St. Mary's Press, 1997.

Joyce, Timothy. Celtic Christianity: A Sacred Tradition, A Vision of
     Hope. NY: Orbis Books, 1998.

Matthews, John. Drinking From the Sacred Well: Personal Voyages of Discovery with The Celtic Saints. CA: HarperSanFrancisco, 1998.

O'Carroll, Brian and Bill Felton. The Story of Clonmacnoise and Saint Ciaran. Ireland: Ely House, 2013.

O'Meara, John J. The Voyage of Saint Brendan: Journey to the Promised Land. Ireland: Dolmen Press, 1981.

Pennick, Nigel. The Celtic Saints: An Illustrated and Authoritative Guide to These Extraordinary Men and Women. NY: Sterling Pub., 1997.

Portaro, Sam. Brightest and Best: A Companion to the Lesser Feasts and Fasts. NY: Cowley Pub., 2001.

Pullen, Bruce Reed. Discovering Celtic Christianity: Its Roots, Relationships, and Relevance. CT: Twenty-Third Pub.,1999.

Sweeney, Jon M. Praying with the Saints. MA: Paraclete Press, 2012.

Tobin, Greg. The Wisdom of St. Patrick: Inspirations from The Patron Saint of Ireland. NY: Falls River Press, 1999.

Waal, Ester de. The Celtic Way of Prayer. The Recovery of the Religious Imagination. NY: Doubleday, 1997.

RESEARCH ONLINE WEB SITES

1. www.newadvent.org

2. www.saintbrendans-online.org

3. www.allsaintsbrookline.org

4. www.lectionarypage.net

5. www.justusanglican.org

6. www.celticlyricscorner.net

7. www.irishcultureandcustoms.com

8. www.irelandseye.com

9. www.kateriirondequoit.org

10. www.oca.org

11. www.maryjones.us

12. www.saintspreserved.com

13. www.goodreads.com

14. wwwchristianityhistoryinstitute.org

15. www.lordsandladies.org

16. www.prayerfoundation.org

17. www.trinitystores.com

18. www.gnosis.org

19. www.marypages.com

20. www.communityofhopeinc.org

21. www.confessio.ie/etexts

ADDITIONAL CELTIC SPIRITUALITY SOURCES

Donohue, John. Anam Cara: A Book of Celtic Wisdom. NY: Cliff
    Street Books, 1997.

- - -. Eternal Echoes: Exploring Our Yearning To Belong. NY: Cliff
Street Books, 1999.

- - -. To Bless the Space Between Us: A Book of Blessings. NY;
    Doubleday, 2008.

Matthews, Caitlin. The Celtic Book of Days: A Guide to Celtic
    Spirituality and Wisdom. Rochester, VT: Destiny Books,
    1995.

- - -. The Celtic Spirit: Daily Meditations for the Turning Year. NY:
    HarperCollins, 1999.

- - -. <u>Celtic Devotional: Daily Prayers and Blessings</u>. MA: Fair
Winds Press, 1996.

MacEowen, Frank. <u>The Celtic Way of Seeing: Meditations on the
Irish Spirit Wheel</u>. CA: New World Library, 2007.

- - -. <u>The Mist-Filled Path: Celtic Wisdom for Exiles, Wanderers,
and Seekers</u>. CA: New World Library, 2002.

Silf, Margaret. <u>Sacred Spaces: Stations on a Celtic Way</u>.MA:
Paraclete Press, 2001.

ABOUT THE AUTHOR

My goal is not only to entertain audiences of all ages through written stories and performance, but also to provide a way for individuals to recapture their imaginations. The realms of fantasy and reality are parted by a thin veil. The timeless truths woven into folk and fairy tales give me this opportunity.

I find great importance in sharing the impact of writing on the human soul. The gentle power of the word heals the wounded heart and uplifts our spirits.

In "The Songweavers' Chronicles," not only are affairs of the heart considered, but I also explore the impact of songs in daily living. Ballads played an important role in ancient Celtic and British societies where balladeers sang of love, country life, hardships, supernatural encounters, court splendors, and folly. Discover their magic!

After reading , please help me spread the word by clicking on the link below where you can **LIKE** and **SHARE** my page with your friends.

www.facebook.com/imaginarylands

NATIONAL AWARD WINNER!

JUST ONE WISH: REALMS OF FAERIE!

Original Faerie tales with fresh twists in narrative poetry for traditional favorites. Celtic settings, magic, mystery - true love shines!

To purchase, visit

www.bobbiepell.com/store.html

Other books available on Amazon by Bobbie Pell

When a woman plans her life, she never includes tragedy.

"Words on a page are powerful." A healing memoir.

Contributing Storyteller. "The Mournful Lady of Binnoire."

Listen to the magical tales of wonder, adventure
and mystery by master storyteller

Bobbie Pell, The Moonstone Minstrel

Take a musical journey to
ancient Celtic lands where
harpers roamed the byways,
seal maidens searched for
lovers, and sailors discover
treasures of the heart.

Discover magical wonders
found in ancient Celtic
lands by meeting kindly
trolls, unusual pipers, and
original stories, poems, and
songs with Celtic motifs.

Master Irish musician
Grey Larsen enhances
each CD with original
improvisations and
traditional O'Carolan
tunes.

**To purchase and join my mailing list for new
book releases, please visit**

www.bobbiepell.com/store.html

Made in the USA
Lexington, KY
22 November 2019